WAKING THE BONES

NEW & SELECTED WORKS

ALAN BIRKELBACH

Texas Review Press
Huntsville, Texas

FIRST EDITION

Requests for permission to acknowledge material from the work should be sent to:

Permissions
Texas Review Press
English Department
Sam Houston State University
Huntsville, TX 77341-2146

ACKNOWLEDGEMENTS: Grateful acknowledgment is to made to the followings books, journals, and magazines in which several of these poems appeared: Poets Laureate of Texas Series, TCU Press; *Weighed in the Balances*; *Meridienne Verte*; *Translating the Prairie*; *Smurglets are Everywhere*; *Rogue Waves*; *Bone Song*; *No Boundaries*; *The Thread*; Poetry Society of Texas Yearbooks (various years); *A Student's Treasury of Texas Poetry*; *The Blue Rock Review*; *Permian Basin Beyond*; *San Pedro River Review*; *Silver Birch*; *Red River Review*; *Illya's Honey*; *Forrest Fest*; *Ardent*; Cowboy Poetry Press/*Unbridled*; *Langdon Review of the Arts*; *8 Voices*; *New Texas*; *Mobius*; *Goodbye Mexico*; *Hunger for Peace Anthology*.

Cover photo © Karla K. Morton

Library of Congress Cataloging-in-Publication Data

Birkelbach, Alan, author.

[Poems. Selections]

Waking the bones : new and selected poems / Alan Birkelbach. -- First edition.

p. cm

Summary: "This is the most complete selection of work by 2005 Texas State Poet Laureate Alan Birkelbach ever put in one volume. It brings together selections that represent his more recognizable pieces, work that has only been available in journals, work that has only been available in books that are out of print or unavailable, plus a generous selection of new work. It represents the period from roughly 1990 to 2015. Stylistically it covers a wide ground, ranging from southwest poetry to children's poetry to a free-verse, narrative voice"--ECIP Summary.

ISBN 978-1-68003-043-3 (paperback : alk. paper)

I. Title.

PS3552.I7543A6 2015

811'.54--dc23

2015024646

For Karla who taught me faith

APOLOGIA

The other day I was talking to a painter that I knew and I made a comment about how her work has changed through the years. It came to the point in the discussion that we explicitly said out loud that we change as artists, life changes us, and sometimes it takes years for us to get the perspective of what we are displaying in our work.

Certainly, my work has changed in the last twenty years. But I rarely go back and try to re-discover what I was thinking at the time. I absolutely refuse to be bound in by a certain style or theme so I am always moving forward. It takes a book like this for me to re-examine thought-processes and terraces of work from five, ten, fifteen years ago.

This volume of New and Selected Works represents my work from roughly 1995 to 2015. As such, it covers a lot of ground. I suppose that if someone were to try and label or categorize my work they would tend to say books like *Rogue Waves* and *Meridienne Verte* fall into one category and then the more southwest poems from *No Boundaries* and *Bone Song* fall into another. But that's generalizing and over-simplifying. I dislike categorization and labels.

I have purposely not put the original publication source on any of the poems listed in this volume. Many of the poems have appeared in multiple places. I am grateful to all publishers and journals who have accepted and printed my work. I have included as complete a list as possible in the acknowledgments.

What I have tried to do was roughly divide the poems into older/published works first and then newer/unpublished works. Within each larger grouping I have tried to divide the non-southwest poems from the southwest poems. There are some groupings I would like to go into more detail on.

You will find a few selections from a book called *Translating the Prairie*. This was actually a book put out by the City of Plano. At the city's request I had written about forty poems about the history of Plano. Each poem was accompanied by artwork created by a citizen of Plano. Unfortunately, in this volume, only a few of the poems are included and none of the art. This book was important because it celebrated a very specific sense of place, an essential part of the thinking of much of Texas letters.

I have also included some selections from my children's poetry book: *Smurglets Are Everywhere*. This book was intended to be written in the style of Jack Prelutsky or Shel Silverstein. Besides the fact that all the poems are in rhyme and meter it is a departure in tone from any of my other work. On the other hand, it represents a pure playful nature that cannot be found in any of my other published work—and for that reason alone it deserves at least small representation.

Also included are some poems from my book called *The Thread* ("From the Spring" and "Numbering".) Again, this was a departure. This book was written entirely from a female point of view. There is a style of book where a narrative, or full story, is told through the use of poetry. This is that type of book. Each poem can stand individually but taken as a whole it presents a story. (Interestingly, at venues, it is one of the books I read from the least. The words, the attitude, the sensibilities do not sound right coming from my mouth. I am waiting for a woman to step forward and perform selections from this book. But even that being said—writing it was worth the risk.)

It would be easy to go into detail on some of the other selections (especially the poems from *Here We Measure Between Wings*) but that level of explanation is probably better suited to another time and place. I welcome that discussion.

Alan Birkelbach

TABLE OF CONTENTS

SELECTED POEMS

NON-SOUTHWEST

SOUTHWEST

SELECTIONS FROM TRANSLATING THE PRAIRIE

SELECTIONS FROM SMURGLETS ARE EVERYWHERE

NEW POEMS

NON-SOUTHWEST

Southwest

Selections from Here We Measure Between Wings

WAKING THE BONES

NON-SOUTHWEST

YOU SHOULD BE HERE, MARIANNE MOORE

,to explain this mystery: a bird
has built his nest in that
mesquite tree yonder. Brave thing, or foolish more like.
Regardless, there's no feline that I
know gaunt enough to squander paws on a misstep.
Too chancy, too slick a bark,

too meager a mouthful for the trip
down. But more, what zephyr
led that bird through mealy, prickly maze? What secret
knowledge was it that guaranteed its
privacy, guarded fledging chicks? What fatigue of
wing? What urgency? What sight?

I saw a telling photo of you
once, Marianne. You were
bent over, furtive almost, standing beside a
herd of elephants, caught in the act,
listening, sagely private, learning ancient rhythms
that the most of us won't know.

I wonder, Marianne: if you joined
me, rocking, on this porch
would you dissemble, twig by twig, for me that nest;
would you describe gentle, grey footfalls;
or would you close your eyes, sigh, rock, and say, "…how the
wizened boards sing, song, sing, song…?"

ROBERT FROST AMONG THE CANNIBALS

It came to me one evening at a reading
as my words fell at the feet of the crowd

that Robert Frost did not meet Death
as well as he might have.

Which is not to say that he did not meet it nobly.
That might have been so. No, I mean, perhaps such a man,

so rich in language, so talented of tongue,
should perhaps have met his end in some fatal last adventure

deep in a jungle, should have had his Nature
meet one final proofing, one ultimate telling scansion.

Dying in bed? Now there's a benign ending.
But preaching a New England drawl to lost savages?

There is saint-like glory of sorts there, regardless of whether those
aboriginals were less concerned about mending walls and snowy woods

than how should they divide the portions and how thick was his leg.
Imagine how after he had finished his recitation

to show their appreciation those cannibals might have risen up and
consumed him whole, all parts, nothing wasted. And, finally, afterwards,

as they gnawed on his bones and sucked his marrow for dessert
They would pat their stretched bellies and say what we already knew,

"Who was that man? The very meat of him was thin and stringy at best.
but oh! Didn't he speak well when he was still alive?"

A BOWL

He carves the kisii stone with the assurance
of someone carving wax. The curls fall back
on his stationery hand; they are cream-colored,
almost albino against his black skin. *Here*, he says,
this elephant is good work, buy this dark one, the one
I am working on, not that light one, that one
does not match your eyes. Instead, though, I favor a large bowl,
purple with many waving lines, soft and warm to
my touch. He smiles, says, *Yes, that bowl,*
I think it has been waiting for you. Why is that, hey?
He puts down the elephant he has been working on.
He puts both my hands inside the bowl
and wraps his flecked hands around them.
Ah, there it is, he says. His eyes glisten.
He gives me a good price. I hold my treasure against my body.

I decide I will write a poem about him.
I find out later—kisii stone is also called soapstone.
Anyone can carve it, even a child. There is no skill
involved.
Everyday when I wake up,
or when I come in from work, the bowl is there, waiting.
Ah, there you are, I say. If I step closer the warmth
washes over me.

When a poet friend drops in unexpectedly
I feed him fruit and nuts from the bowl.
Ah, there you are, I say.
Let's trade poems.

FALLING IN

It's when something develops a hole unexpectedly
that you have to start watching.

It's not like the pinching and unpinching of a clothespin
she thought. When she bent down to the bag of pins
the blood rushed to the bruise in her cheek, making her squint,
making her focus more firmly on the thought.
It was like your Grandma who one day is baking pies,
the juicy apple ones with the fork pricks for an edge,
and the next day she's just sitting pale and senseless on the flower sofa
calling you by your brother's name, her eyes focusing on nothing.

One day you are twenty and your man stares so long at you
that it makes you feel uncomfortable and good at the same time
and every morning, yes, every morning, you wake up with him
and you can actually see definition on his delts and glutes
and you thank somebody, anybody, that life is so nice and tightly strung.
Then, say, one day, he gets up before you get a chance to look
and the chain gets broken.
Maybe that fruitless mulberry in the backyard
is torqued by the wind just enough and now instead of growing true and up
one limb twists and now there's a sumpy pocket that holds water.
Maybe some anonymous farmer when he climbed from his field onto the road
accelerated too fast on his tractor in a dinosaur kind of way
and one errant tine from the rake dragged all squimpy along the bar ditch,
making a line aching for erosion later.

One of her arms still hurt so she used the other one
to lift the weight of the sheet onto the line.
It's like a surprise; you can't plan for it.
You expect things to turn one way and for some reason,
this time, maybe from now on, they don't.
You keep the bugs off the tomatoes, you give them lots of water.
They look fine when you go to bed, and the next morning
there's a chasm big enough for a finger
and you can see all the veins and seeds inside.
One day you put too much sugar in the ice tea
or you don't iron the shirt quite right
and that open fist swings around when you aren't looking.

Weld, patch, concrete, fill, moan, pray, cry over it all you want.
The integrity of it's gone. So, what do you do?
You try to watch your step a little more but you know now
it doesn't do any good and why didn't anyone teach this lesson, huh?
Wisdom sounds kinda like whimsy but they aren't the same.
Next thing you know you are hanging clothes on a clothesline
working around the bruises.
Next thing you know a sinkhole
forms in the middle of a street and trucks start falling in,
water begins draining in that direction,
cool air starts blowing out,
people find bones at the bottom,
and at night the bats queue up.

THE SEPARATION OF THE SEASONS

I have begun to think of you as a pumpkin
     and that frightens me.
I dread that there must be a cut, drying, green vine
  somewhere close by   yearning.
I know that this is way we used to sleep
  but I can't lay my ear on your chest anymore
  because I will hear the faint wind moving
  the moist, fibrous strings and seeds aside.
I think that one day, or maybe two,
  I won't remember to look
  but when I do I'll find your cheeks shrunken,
    more and deeper furrows around the cavities.
If there were room for a candle
    it would be burning low.

This season is too long.
I wish for the chill of Winter for you.
I cannot stand this long, drawn-out Octobering.

THE FORMER POET LAUREATE SAID

that he had finally just had enough
of admirers puttering down the sidewalk

onesy, twosy, like lost flagellants,
with copies of his books in their hands.

They were always mewling and whiny, waiting
for him to appear on his stoop

to "bless you, bless you all."
He admitted he was too accessible.

When he was younger inspiration
was as common as meatloaf.

He could pretty much rub two sticks together
and make a poem out of it.

But the reality was that one day his Muse
died inside him and he was left to try and hold

his reputation together on momentum alone.
It wasn't, he said, so much a matter of losing control

as having control getting up and taking a flight
one-way to Bolivia or some other godforsaken place

where it's probably struggling right now
inside some mustached coffee-picker

who owns one shirt and two goats and whose
entire vocabulary rhymes with "sangria."

But I noticed that even as he talked
he worked the chicken on the grill

and between the turning of each breast
there was an unspoken, counted pause

and the lines were laid in regular rows
that he would constantly write and rewrite.

FINDING A WOODEN LEG IN THE ROAD

It did not seem like
something that should be lost.

It was too perfect a thing, bondage gleaming and attached,
grain swirled and jointed,

all carved toes and painted nails,
nubbed, worn and chipped up to the calf.

It rested quietly against the curb,
not drawing attention to itself,

like a tired can or beaten newspaper;
my eye had just happened on it as I walked.

It was as heavy and strange to my hands as a step-child,
full of ghost aches and pains.

Had it fallen from some careless pickup loaded with miscellany,
(perhaps a theft from some house, grabbing all unsecured items)?

Did someone cavalierly toss it aside because he had extra,
because there was a newer model, more life-like, more attractive?

Was there dancing in the middle of a wish-filled night,
as that lost limb, like a lizard, grew back?

Had someone adopted a leaning life,
now bound to long skirt and overcoat instead of a foreign stick?

Or, if I listened closely would I hear,
a block or closer away, a rhythmic scuffing

as of someone fretting on his overworked heel,
wondering, wondering....

WARNING! DO NOT LET YOUR NON-POET FRIENDS READ YOUR POETRY!

They will tell you it is good.
But they mean "good" as in "not bad,"
as in "it stayed on the page like it should,"
and "it looks artsy with no rhyme and all."

But that "good" is not even as strong as a house is "good" and safe.
Something can taste "good" and feel "good"
like cold water on a searing day
or hot soup out of the blizzard's reach
but that 'good' isn't even that nurturing.

That "good" is for when you are five
and leaving Suzy Sutkin's party
and your collar is buttoned up to your neck
and your mother makes you say
"Thank you I had a good time,"
when you really didn't.

It is a "good" mixed with a vacuous stare;
it is bland like old pudding;
it is a small, old dog
who sheds quietly in your lap.

But sometimes I want my poetry to be a bad dog
that will not sit or stay, that has not lost its bark,
a cur, uneven and ragged.

When you read it I want it to back you up
against the wall.
With each line I want it to nip and snarl at your legs,
lips pulled back and specked gums showing with each phrase
so you can see its teeth that you think
are going to sink into your arms
down to the cold bone.
And I want your forehead to sweat
and your face to wash
and your blood to turn so pale and still
that my poem will drift from your fingers
and come to rest, still snarling,
against your torn and tattered shoes.

ABOUT CANNIBALS

About cannibals I have very little to say.
It is one of those topics you will rarely see
a poem written about.

I do not know any cannibals I am aware of,
and, by extension, I do not think my friends know any either.

I brought the question up to my druggist, my dentist,
and my twice-a-month therapist and none of them
knew personally any cannibals.

Then I asked a man I didn't know:
some blood-stained guy down at the fish market,
wearing a leather hat,
a horrible filet knife hanging from his belt,
with a scar along his jaw-line,
and he said, "Aw, sure, I know a bunch of 'em.'

"And, hey mister, if you want a good red snapper
I can wrap one up. Otherwise, sorry, gotta go."
Then with a hook, and just one hand,
he flung a forty pound tuna across the room,
swearing at the receiving lug who did not catch it.

I went home that night,
and, there in the darkness of the backyard,
as my wife and I sat and watched the stars,
I asked her if she knew any cannibals.
She sighed and said,
"There are too many stars out there
for me to think about cannibals."

AFTER JUDGING A TEENAGE POETRY CONTEST

This beer should be refreshing—
but all I can think about
is a teenage girl somewhere within the city-state of Troy,
who, having just taken a look at the big wooden horse,
is now back in her room,
pining and moaning,
wondering whether a boy will ever love her
the way that other boy loved Helen.
Maybe he would lay siege to a city for her.

The breeze here in my backyard tries soothing away
some of my squint lines, tries to reassure me that
I am alone with my thoughts,
but no, drifting across the yard floats
the image of a spectral boat,
and from the back seat comes
chilly, echoing monotones
of Charon's daughter who's saying she will
never get a new dress if all her father charges
is two coins a ride.

Far off, in distant invisible woods,
I can hear a woodpecker, following his nature,
tap-tap-tapping, searching for elusive insects.
And then I am reminded about an
asymmetrical mishap of a poem
where in the space of twenty-eight unscannable lines
the poet used the word 'forever' twelve times.

I should have brought something to eat,
something crunchy, some comfort food,
something to undo this knot in my jaw—
but when I think of food it triggers
the thought of a young girl who's been wandering
around the desert for years
and now she has flumphed down
and is letting the world know
how she wants fresh manna, right now,
not something from this morning.
If her friends saw her coming with stale manna
why she might as well run off into the wilderness.
By herself.

It is certainly heart-rending to think
that somewhere in the distant past
a Pictish princess was compelled
to fight against the Romans
when it was perfectly obvious that her skin
was not the proper shade of blue.

And while Romeo and Juliet were a little over-wrought
they at least had the decency
to wrap things up in three acts.
We should also give credit to Pyramus and Thisbe
who were fated to be eaten by lions.
And then there are the innumerable lovers
that Ovid wrote of, changing into trees,
and fish, and cows, and whatnot.
At least they aren't writing poems anymore.

But there are always more young poets
than there are timely metamorphoses.
And those poets demand to be heard.
Which probably explains the walking journeys of Basho.
He treasured each step,
and counted them in short forms,
fully aware that back home,
behind thin silk panels,
interminably miffed at being left behind,
his daughter obviously had
so much more to say.

AND WHAT COMES NEXT

"Act as if it were impossible to fail"
Dorothea Brande

There are mornings of course
when failure is already pre-ordained.
I have heard there is the divining art

that allows certain people to read the swirls
of milk as it pours into coffee.
This morning I swear I acted as if I would

successfully pour the milk into my coffee.
I have done it without failure,
both privately and in public, again and again,

but today, in my bleariness,
when I poured the milk into my coffee
the little swirls made a picture

of what I think was Doris Day
when her hair was pulled up high,
like maybe when she was in a Rock Hudson movie

or in *The Pajama Game*. And then I had to wonder
why Doris Day would appear to me.
Other people get visitations from dead relatives

or, even better, our Lady of Guadalupe
(although I understand that Lady prefers
the almost gel-fixative qualities of latte foam.)

At least with a dead relative or Lupe
there is a certain amount of expectation
that the visitant has an inside track

about knowledge from the other side
And you really have to bow down to that.
I mean, you just have to.

But with Doris Day I had to ponder
what the rest of the day was going to bring.
Of course I had failed in pouring milk into the coffee

because now I could not stir it,
I could not make little cyclones of Doris Day's face.
It wouldn't have been right.

What other small exquisite failures were awaiting me?
Would the bite of my teeth
into my cheap baked pastry

turn into a perfect scalloping
that would easily line up, curve for curve,
for the shell that ferried Venus?

When I brushed my hair as I was drying it,
something I swear I have done several thousand times
with certainly passing-grade results,

would I somehow end up with a perfect Elvis curl,
as if some spirit was channeled,
and I needed blue suede shoes to get through the day?

Or, finally, as I bent to put on my brown oxfords,
the well-worn ones, who have served me as friends
through puddles and weddings—

yes, those brown oxfords—
would I fail miserably in their tying,
my fingers developing an unexplained, routed, twitch

as they twined the lace into a perfectly artistic, historically accurate
Gordian knot,
designed to make sure

my shoe never left my foot,
no matter how far I walked,
no matter how stiff they looked every night in bed?

LET ME SETTLE IN, BETWEEN THE LITTLE HILLS

At night, as I try to go to sleep,
I imagine myself
lying in the sand, fresh out of the surf.
I do not need you yet.
I try to settle myself on the sheets,
between the little quilted squares of the mattress,
my hips, my elbows, my wrists, my ankles
finding the little indentions, me measured out,
in little sewn squares, gridded, slotted in.
I imagine myself like I was lying on the beach,
the curves of me searching for brown curves.
There is a roar in my ears. It seems to get louder
the closer to sleep I get. And my body finds
the little indentions where it is supposed to be, its spots.
And I rest my head on my arm, like a pillow.
And here is where I need you. I think of you
forming around me like a blanket of sun,
until there is nothing next to me that isn't warm.
Or maybe, later, you can be the sheet of moonlight,
scarf-like in a breeze and gauzy,
and you will be pulled up
just high enough,
so my shoulders are exposed, bare and salty,
to your lips.

LEVEL OF DETAIL

*According to NASA there is verifiable, empirical,
photographic evidence of cyclones occurring on Mars.*

Mr. Dad Martian, not ten minutes earlier,
had been cooling his eight very green and tired legs
in a Martian plastic baby pool

while Mrs. Mom Martian, her wiry and crystalline hair
still in a 'do' fresh from church,
was busy flipping burgers on the stove,

when in the heat of the Sunday Martian afternoon
the cyclone had dropped down out of that iron oxide sky.
It had started into spinning the legs

of the little wooden-yard-art Martian ducks.
Then, in a show of real disrespect,
it commenced to whipping the tar out of the Martian civil war flags

that were hanging over the entrance to the trailer park.
Like it had eyes that twirling monster started
ripping up mailboxes, one by one.

It popped the clotheslines, bent the cable dishes,
knocked over birdbaths,
and plucked all the avocado-colored plastic daisies.

Little Martian dogs barked their two heads
almost soundlessly in the thin air
before they were lifted up and away.

And all Mr. Dad Martian really had time to see
before his cousin's barbecue pit
was deposited three craters over

was Grandma Martian hurrying up the driveway,
dropping her canes, suddenly cured of being lame,
all her arms and antennae waving in panic.

LIVING ALONE

Tonight for dinner
I believe I will eat over the sink.
Something that has lots of crumbs.
Maybe crackers. Or a very flaky pastry.

Afterwards I intend to not mop
and not vacuum. Although just this morning
I stepped barefooted
on something dark and nubbly in the kitchen.
I picked it up and then didn't wash my hands immediately.

Tonight I will steal more than my half of the blanket.
My toes will untuck the sheets,
both upper and lower ones.
The chances are good I will also claim all the pillows.

When I am working in the yard tomorrow
I will not use sun screen.
I will swat at circling bees. I will not wear a hat.

I will take time out, at any given moment,
to go inside and watch a golf tournament on T.V.
I will turn down the volume and just watch them swing.
I may also decide to watch a movie
I have already seen five times.

For a snack I will read the labels of food in the pantry
and find the one that has the highest
carb and fat counts. And eat too much of that.

I will nap without setting an alarm.

And, just so you will know,
in case you ever read this:

tomorrow morning
I intend to put butter on
only half of my toasted English muffin,

and taking my coffee
with way too much cream,
which you also did not like.

LUNCH WITH THE MAENADS

Once Eurydice got used to the idea
that Orpheus had premature issues

she was able to reconcile some things.
It took time of course. The Gods love drama

so she went through months of just drinking asphodel wine.
After that she obsessively mapped and named

every grotto and stalactite-filled chamber she could find.
Then she went pescatarian—would only eat blind fish.

Eventually she settled down, made friends with Persephone,
flirted, but only in a good way, with Hades.

Until, finally, the Gods had decided that healing was done
so they let Eurydice and Persephone have lunch

within a high, charming little stony alcove,
just out of the light's reach,

that looked down on wonderful bucolic fields
that Eurydice had almost forgotten still existed.

And since the Gods are ultimately ironic,
the entertainment for the day,

there on those fields lush with green,
fervor-filled, splattered here and there

with tiny charming outcroppings of loose stones,
the entertainment for the day was the Maenads

tormenting Orpheus, shouting curses even as he sang.
Persephone remarked while she nibbled on cress,

"It is good to be so removed.
I cannot hear that awful screeching at all."

"Hmmmm," Eurydice answered, watching
as the Maenads began hurling sticks

that hung lazily in the air, seduced by the song.
She half expected she would shed a tear when

the wild women began to hurl rocks,
some eventually tearing through the spell

and gashing her former lover's head,
but the sweetmeats on her stone plate were distractingly exquisite.

"Why look," Persephone said,
"They have quite torn off his head—

and still he continues to sing!"
Eurydice barely tilted her pale head as if to listen—

then dabbed at an invisible morsel around her mouth.
After all, those figures were so far off

and the song so removed
that it barely trembled her keen, obsidian knife.

NEGATIVE CONFESSIONS

If you're keeping track
(and several theologian friends tell me you are)
I did not leave a can
of donated vegetables for the Boy Scouts.

One time I told my dog I would give her a treat
if she would just stop barking—
and she did—but I didn't.
I didn't give my dog a treat. There. I said it.

The other day I didn't pour hot water
on an ant bed instead of chemicals.
One afternoon while shopping
I did not use a recycled bag.

But why am I bringing these up?
If you've been paying attention
you know I am not ambitious
when it comes to sinning.

Are you getting all this down?
Or do you have a legion of angels
working away in little carols like monks
who are assigned the task of transcribing,

through some heavenly machine,
every sin we act out,
miniscule to huge,
even the ones we didn't think were sins,

like not feeding the pigeons.
or not inflating our tires,
or not chewing all bites
at least twenty times.

I probably should have bought some indulgences
but I did not. I bought lotto tickets.
and a little pine cone air freshener
that will hang from the rear view mirror

on the off chance that if doomsday comes
one day while I am driving
I will at least go smelling nice and minty.
Just like a saint.

Okay. Vanity then. I'll give you that one.
But just look at the things I haven't done.
I haven't forgotten my Grammie on her birthday.
I haven't pushed the elevator button more than once.

And one last thing: this morning I did not mow the lawn.
I'm not exactly sure who that is a sin against
but I know I didn't do it
so I just thought I would mention it.

PLEASE WRITE BACK

This poem is to reply to all those people
who have been expecting a letter from me
and have never received it.
This includes all of you who have been expecting
thank you notes. Even from my first marriage.
I do not remember who gave me the candlesticks
but I am sure I treasured them always.
They looked beautiful on my table
(I'm sure I had a table once.)

This letter is also intended for all those speakers
who visited my school during National Poetry month
and encouraged us to write an epistle poem
to someone we would never normally
write a letter to. At the time I think I wrote it to Barbara Eden
but based on results it appears to never have arrived.
I should have tried someone more to the point,
more literature-based,
like Shakespeare or Sappho or Frost.
If someone is dead you do not expect them to write back anyway.
They will never get smarter and will never try to
over-impress you with their wisdom. It just won't happen.

And this letter is also to
all those pen pals I should have corresponded with.
I am especially apologetic to the pen pal from Germany
who sent such beautiful snapshots
of the countryside where he lived.
I sent him one of my school photos
and a picture I drew of my cat.
My only consolation and hope is that I know
I have changed considerably
since the second grade. I am at least somewhat taller.

And finally, I do not anticipate I will be sending out
creative and scrap-booked invitations
to any type of party,
be it birthday, anniversary, retirement, or solstice.
Quite frankly, I do not have the time,
nor do I have drawers full of the requisite
stamps, decals, and cut-out foam symbols.
I am obviously far behind on my correspondence
and my hand can only be expected to do so much.

RECALCULATING

There is no Royal Road to Geometry.
I could have told Ptolemy that.

Having survived the curriculum-and-ruler-based
Mrs-Zankers-sixth-grade-math-class

I am fairly convinced no cartographer
has ever charted a Royal Road to Geometry.

Having said there is no ROYAL road
the implication is there is a road somewhere

(hidden though it may have been
from clueless and fearful sixth graders.)

I have heard of the Road to Perdition,
The Road to Hell, and the Appian Way.

I have heard of The Mother Road, Abbey Road,
and the Boulevard Saint-Germain.

Those are the easy ones, perfect answers for trivia games.
There are at least a score of others.

I do harbor a certain level of curiosity
about the dress code for these trips,

especially for the Road to Ruin,
and what type of accommodations

one can expect when they get there.
For instance, The Mother Road calls for t-shirts,

and the Road to Hell, or so I imagine at least,
would demand something too gaudy, too glittery, or too transparent.

It seems like the Road to Ruin, though, could be a quick trip.
One minute rubies and the next minute rocks.

It would be hard to chart, hard to anticipate,
hard to visualize the rills, canyons, and peaks.

How do you dress for the trip?
Do you pack Ruined Scarves, Ruined Slacks, Ruined Silk Pajamas?

It makes one wonder how to prepare,
makes one visualize the hotel at the other end:

the tiles cracked in the lobby,
glass dropping from the chandeliers,

wallpaper peeling from the walls,
the tub long past redeeming.

You can't even begin to imagine how you ever got here,
how many hours it might take you to get home.

RISK

I tell everyone else to take risks
but I prefer to hide behind my in-the-moment words.
I have always had a problem
with poets who confess what they are feeling.

Especially considering the fact that
I believe each poem is a contract
where the poet has to convince the reader
the poem belongs to both of them.

Well, that's love then, isn't it?
some of my romantic friends say,
which prompts them into nuzzling in public
which can get ugly really quickly.
It's like writing poetry. You have to
know when to stop.

See what I did there? I diverted,
turned it into a moment again.
But everything is a series of moments
It's all because we're self-aware.
We think every space we walk through
we instantly make important.

Confession was good enough for St. Augustine
so I should be willing to accept it
from other less talented (and less saint-like) poets.

It's a risk this laying oneself open.
Years ago my father took two old truck hoods
and welded them together.
Then on one end, for a seat,
he bolted a plywood plank
onto a caged, empty, twenty-gallon can.

It was the ugliest boat ever
but it could not be turned over
and all he wanted to do was fish
on a quiet river. That's all.

There's another hobby that's in the moment:
Fishing. It always depends on the x, y, and z
of intersecting time, fish, and bait.
We always hope the fish are waiting for us.
We want to enter into a contract.

Again I have side-stepped. Years ago,
in a moment of what I thought was foresight,
I learned to dance. As it turns out—it is not a skill
like riding a bicycle. You can forget.

But fishing, writing, confessing, dancing—
It's all taking a risk.
You have to be shown how
even if you don't know the name for it
or all the mechanics.

Like my father.
He would walk down the path to the river
and throw the cooler and rods
and bait and net and oar into the boat.
Then he would unlock it from its chain
and step in.
He would use the oar to push off from the bank
And he would back up
and sit down on that little square platform.
A smile would cross his face.
He would take a deep breath,
then he would paddle away,
and it was obvious he felt
positively buoyant.

SEMI-COLON

*According to some scholars, the semi-colon is about to go the way of Pluto. It may
be taken off the list of 'official' punctuation marks. It no longer aligns with
current language usage and requirements. Its usage is so subtle as to make it
almost indistinguishable from a colon or comma.*

I do worry about the extra duty
this is going to put
on the comma and the period,
both of which are
already over-worked.

My grammar book goes on
for ten pages about
the proper use of the semi-colon.
Of course, that book was written
before this declaration was made.

It will be like Roman numerals
or cursive hand-writing,
shining our own shoes.
We used to think these essential,
things we had to know.

I'm just saying:
declaring Pluto is no longer a planet
is not going to stop
all grade-school-mnemonic-rhymes.
He's still out there, hanging around,
exerting his pull on other bodies.

But not much pull.
Just like the semi-colon—
who is not as muscular
or terminal as a period.

The semi-colon can't finish off
the sentence with a flourish,
(consider the exclamation point!)

but he's perfect
for the inside work,
the lists of things,
the trim.

It's barely there.
It's a little more breath than a comma,
slightly bigger metaphorically
than an asteroid,
not as large as a question mark.

It isn't like a semi-colon
has much of an albedo
but it definitely has mass.

Just try to remove it
from a sentence
and see
how the gravity
falls apart.

THE CHOLERA EPIDEMIC OF 1817

I have chosen that particular epidemic
because I have found a picture of it,
although I am sure I could find other less grisly charts.
According to this illustration, it appears that
little red arrows started up in the Ganges
and, according to this footnote,
worked their way north and west
at the nonchalant rate of five miles a day
until finally reaching Paris
which evidently was the bulls-eye.

Granted, cultural and scientific understanding
of reading signs has changed over generations,
but it seems to me that even the folks of 1817
might have been a little suspicious
when giant red arrows slowly started stretching their way
across the rows and cart-paths,
and every place they touched the people got cholera.

It doesn't take a genius at extrapolation
to try and anticipate where the arrows are headed,
especially if they are only moving at approximately
eighteen feet a minute (give or take).
Even the most moronic peasant
could do a line of sight at that rate
and determine that, yup, in a few hours it
would probably be best to avoid the village.

Maybe they acted like their
counterparts from a few centuries earlier
who might have shouted,
"The Black Death!" or
"Here Comes Alexander and he's conquering!"
or "Watch out for the little ice age!"

I can only assume that scientists and historians
have studied other charts
and tried to determine the origins
of these giant red arrows.
They seem to only appear when there's
sweeping waves of disease, tragedy, or movement.

Sometimes all at once.

I have since seen another chart
of how a black hole works
and there those arrows were again.
In this scenario it seems they were taking all light
and time with them
as they disappeared into a funnel shape.

Their rate of travel was much faster
than five miles a day.
Acceleration and momentum and friction
do not seem to constrain them much.

The newspaper today printed an article
that illustrated how the part of the country I live in
has become suddenly more attractive
because of the economy, climate, and erudition,
(I added that last one.)

There was an accompanying chart
that attempted to show the influx of people
from far states, and even other countries.
Giant red arrows seemed to be pointing
at my town, if not my neighborhood.
I could detect no explanatory note
about rate of travel.

I hope I have time to move.

THE DEAD LETTER DEPARTMENT

Sometimes it comes down
to the facts we think we know.

Like in winter how most of our body heat
escapes through our head.
Or how we can see
the Great Wall of China from space.
Just like we all know
that the Catholic Church got rid of a bunch of their saints.
Well, we don't know exactly when—
but we all know it happened.
It was like one day there were
too many saints in the sock drawer,
and some of them just didn't match up anymore,
and suddenly—poof—there were fewer in the basket.

It's a myth of course.
All the saints were still there.
Some saints just got their feast days taken away.

Well, once word got out it was clear
there would be no more
demanding the day off for St. Cornelius
(the patron saint against twitching).
And there certainly wouldn't be a search
for a candelaria for St. Januarius
(the saint of volcanic eruptions).

But without a Feast Day
then you can't spend the whole day thinking about it,
about how much thanks you owed to St. Zita,
(the saint for waiters).
And how certainly you were breathlessly
planning a menu to celebrate St. Anthony of Egypt
(the saint of gravediggers).

The demarcation must have made
some type of distinction in Heaven,
a line down the middle of the canonization club house,

a new degree of veneration,
"You can believe in these folks' stories—
but those…not so much.
But we're sure they're still a swell bunch of guys."

There were still plenty of saints to go around,
but with these gaps it made years of pious thinking seem,
I don't know, misspent? Now we would all have to
to stop in the middle of the day,
any common day, and remember to thank St. Peregrine,
for keeping us away from running sores.

It used to be we had a whole day for that, just for him,
just to think about it.

But now, this is our life.
We sit at our tables, raising our glasses,
rubbing against new holy elbows,
and say to ourselves, "Yes, this is just as good."
And even then our old Saints are tapping at the window,
saying let us in, we are so hungry.
We just look outside,
while we gnaw on the turkey legs,
and say, with our mouths full,
"What are you even doing here?
Didn't you get our note?"

THE PARKED EMPTY RAILROAD CARS ON THE RURAL TRACKS

There was a reasoning mind that left them here,
doors open to the wind, still life with no hobos.

The track in both directions must go somewhere,
places they had probably been before, both ways,

if they had the metallic sense to think or memorize.
But they were just dragged here and left, unhooked, and nothing.

We could climb into them if we wanted.
No one would say anything.

We imagined if we could leave pieces of ourselves
on empty tracks like this

then we could have just abandoned our twenties, or thirties,
a few bad months of our lives,

lost the paperwork, said the switch going down there
had rusted out of position, parked the cars way out of sight.

People could look through them, like exhibits,
like we looked at trapped animals looking back through glass.

Those people could learn all there was about us.
And that's why we don't climb up.

It's too much like those pictures of graveyards full of airplanes,
ghosts tangling in the propellers, falling out the bomb doors,

young spirits laying back in the shattered turrets,
praying to be set free.

VISITING HEAVEN

If we are going to go to the trouble
of constructing all these religions
then we might as well
have a have firm idea of what the afterlife is like.

It's not like vacation.
There are no photos of the resort,
the circling driveway, the grandiose check-in desk,
the infinity pool.

We might like to imagine it would be
way better than a timeshare,
the type of place where the bellboy already knows your name,
and if there's a mint on your pillow,
and you eat it,
then another mint would be there—just like that.

There would be the ubiquitous smell of piña colada—
unless you don't like piña colada.
in which case it's something else.
There is a steward always handy when you need him.
His name is always Hay-zus.
He will bring you a free drink
that you have already paid for.

Funny thing about religion:
we didn't begin with the end in mind
when we constructed the artifice.

Maybe Heaven is like a poem,
or more like the idea of a poem.
Free will with words. Will we be formalists
or do we choose to spread syllables helter-skelter
across the page? And what's the target?
Can we ever approach that perfect vanishing point,
that combination of sounds that suddenly makes us ascend?

I'd like to think that Adam was a poet.
He didn't have much to write about until Eve showed up—
then the whole love poetry thing snowballed.
For them, Heaven was simple:

Open the back door.
The leaflets in the mail from all the local churches
hadn't started arriving yet,
cable T.V. was a few years off,
and neighbors were limited to wildebeests.
A day there would go like this:
Eve, probably totally naked,
would plant herbs and fruits and vegetables

and all manners of flowers,
some in rows and some not so much—
"—just for effect—".
Adam would sit on a lounge,
rudimentary pencil and paper in hand,
watching Eve and her pendulous breasts,
and decide he just had to thank somebody.

I bet their back yard
smelled just like coconuts.

VOICE-OVER

There, on the documentary,
how comical the lion looked.

Almost like a cartoon,
when she sat down
and hung onto the gazelle with one paw.

With the other paw I imagined her
scratching behind her ear,
or checking her nails,
or drinking a glass of wine,
or reading *Variety*.

The narrator of the documentary said
that if the gazelle could once free herself
from that hindering paw
then her speed would let her completely escape.

That all depended, of course,
my argumentative mind said,
on the lion suddenly deciding
to wave with both paws at a best-friend girlfriend lion
just there across the veldt.
Or maybe she would be humming an old catchy tune
and decided impulsively to clap along.

The narration had the artifice of a sporting event
where there is a voice pumping up
our anticipation of a perfect putt for instance,
with something anecdotal added about the ease of stroke
and practiced eye.

Only in the movies is there a voice-over
for the fumbled intricacies of a first kiss
or for a description of the particular angle
of an open elbow that powers the whiskey
pouring down a throat.

I am not sure that a narrator
could add much drama to the tableau of
the rabbit that sneaks into my yard at night
to eat my lettuce.
And I am not even sure that sonorous tones
could augment the emotional landscape
of the shadowy murder of crows
that descends into the grocery store parking lot
for no apparent reason other than group discussion.

And I truly do not anticipate
that several years from now,
or maybe next week,
there will be a camera crew
and a gravelly whispering observer somewhere close by
when I wander far off track
and find myself in the situation
where Death has a hold of my belt in one hand
and with the other hand
he tries unsuccessfully
to stifle a yawn.

ULTIMATELY

Linnaeus believed in the Grand Design. In his system there was no mechanism of
change because God designed all organisms perfectly the first time.
The Day The Universe Changed, James Burke

Having spent the last twenty minutes
trying to untangle the conical wire tomato cages
and realizing in a taxonomic, evolving kind of way
they are related to coat hangers,

I sit here now on a hot metal lounge chair on the patio
sipping a beer and realizing with no little pride
that I fought the many-spindly-legged beast
to a standstill.

It is at moments like this, sweaty and slightly inebriated,
my brain swerves towards phrases and metaphors.
Linnaeus, straight man that he was,
wouldn't have liked the word swerve.

Perhaps I would mention to him the taunting squirrels
who have not learned their place in this grand scheme.
Or the lizard who has learned to visit my front door to remind me
if I don't sweep the dead bugs he will take care of it.

That might not be enough to set Linnaeus spinning.
So I will mention that evidently God did not design
the wear and tear clause in my lease. Nor did the Almighty
have a finger on the depreciation of my car.

And I suspect it wasn't him who made me buy
the magic rotisserie-oven off late-night T.V.
that broke ten minutes after I got it out of the box.
Linnaeus—I am not done.

God is also probably not the mind behind
"new and improved stickers." Granted, He might be the one
who has helped me be content with the piles of laundry I accumulate—
the whole reverting to a natural state thing--but probably not.

Yet, Linnaeus, I still believe that everything has its place.
Currently, my butt belongs in this hot lawn chair.
And this beer belongs in my hand.
The tangled snarl of tomato cages belongs on the other side of the yard.

There's an order here, a balance—my own personal Versailles.
And even so, when the squirrels dig holes willy-nilly,
and the tomatoes die an untethered death,
there will still be more than enough blame to go around.

VERITAS

Truth lies in the bottom of wells
Old Greek Proverb

If you read most how-to-write books
almost all of them will tell you to keep a journal.
What they do not say is that it should be pink,
with a tiny little lock, (with a bendy little key),
and there should be a poodle on the cover
with sequins for a collar.
Or maybe that is a diary. Besides, no writer
I know actually writes in a journal. They just tell everyone else
to do it. They may have several blank journals,
pages they definitely intend to fill up later.
If you ask them they will swear to it.

Maybe the old Greeks should have said
that truth lies in the bottom of sock drawers,
the lint trap on the dryer,
the tackle box you never cleaned out
(with dried worms on rusty hooks.)
Remember: you voluntarily bought that exercise machine.
Do you remember where you put the instruction manual?
That place would be overflowing
with the untapped sweat of truth.

It's a catalog—all the places truth could be hiding.
Like one day your kids will find the old photos of you,
pre-braces, with the bad haircut, and the plaid shorts,
and they will wonder what else they don't know.
And you'll laugh with them—but after they leave
you'll bury that box a little deeper.

And you'll start thinking about
where you have put other pieces.
And you'll say "thank god I never wrote in a journal,"
but truth is already ahead of you,
sifting dust in the attic,
reading your old love letters.
Or maybe truth is finding and leaving out on the table
that library book from high school
you always intended to return.

You start finding some mornings
are thinner and less secure than others.
Sometimes, like your own mother,
you will take your coffee black.
Sometimes you will almost swear
there was a message in that darkness.

And sometimes you will worry,
laugh, but still worry,
that a tiny skull will bob to the surface,
Its jaws spreading open
ready to speak your name.

LOSING OUR WATCHES AT THE BEACH

When we get there
we put them in a drawer,
a conscious effort
to make ourselves lose track.

We unload the clothes quickly,
stock the pantry and fridge,
squirrel away the boxes,
arrange the books we plan to read.

Then swallow the rest of the day
like it was spilling unending from a well,
always coming—
we are there to drink it.

We cook dinner
timed by our bellies.
Watch the moon's trail
for permission to sleep.

Turn over the alarm clock,
depending on the sun
and body warmth
to wake up.

And at five-thirty a.m.
as if nudged,
I wake up anyway,
reaching for my glasses and a pen

I try rolling over,
cursing the words away,
a part of me already hearing iambs
in the breakers dicing outside.

Eyes wide open,
all things clear,
I start a villanelle
from the ceiling fan's circling.

Lying on the sheet
my hand flexes into a tiny O,
pushing, pulling,
forming phantom words.

My toes start beating syllables.
My wife prods me with her hip.
"The coffee is set up.
Just turn it on."

I kiss her cheek,
slide from the bed, lines falling
into place before my feet
touch slippers.

There's a clock in my bones I can't deny,
the monk-weight of motes and water,
burning as sure as a candle, driven by sounds,
the number of breaths through a night.

NUMBERING

After our husbands had gone off to work
we would go to each other's house in the mornings
still in bathrobes or house-slippers
(nothing frilly—we realized the fire
of the mornings was just a memory of a reflection—
we remembered what it looked like and smelled like—
and even though some words say
that objects in mirror are closer than they appear
those words lie.)
Sometimes we sorted through cards, planned dinners,
compared shampoos. Mostly
we just confessed. We exchanged invisible veils,
whispered and listened through
only slightly obscuring lattices of coffee steam.
One day she admitted to me, half-laughing,
that on some especially empty nights,
when he was already in bed but she was still up
maybe ironing or sorting clothes
she would take the car
and drive through the neighborhood
with no other purpose other
than counting dogs.
She would roll down the window and cruise
slowly on a circuit, her arm hanging just outside
on the paint of the door.
Just a bark would not qualify, she said smiling.
It had to be the whole dog, loose, out hunting
or sniffing or doing a doggie thing. She would
find one, point her finger and count, "One."
See another—say, "Two." And so on.
Sometimes the dogs would look up, be surprised,
tilted their heads, tentatively wag their tails.
Sometimes they would be full-maned and showing teeth.
Some nights there were several in a pack, a regular
doggie convention—all of them counted.

It reassured her somehow but she didn't understand why.
She could come back home with a number
and she could go to bed with it and hold on it.
You must think I'm crazy, she said.
No, not at all I said, we all need something
and I would hug her,
then we would move on to the recipe for great pancakes.
But that day she added another item
to my list of wishes:
I started hoping
that on the nights when he didn't have an
especial lot to do, and maybe Mrs. God was already asleep,
that maybe God drove through the neighborhood at night
in, I don't know, maybe a cloud-gray Bonneville,
and he would look through the walls into the houses
into the living rooms into the bedrooms
(because, after all, he IS God)
and he would see people like me, sitting there,
in the dark,
and he would smile
and point his finger out the window
and say, "One…"

WHEN GOD GETS UP IN THE MORNING

I would bet he usually gets up before
even the chickens he created.

Does he yawn, huge and widely majestic,
his roar tearing down dreamy mountains?

Does he slide along the hallway in his worn slippers,
willing on lights as he goes?

I wonder if he likes just plain coffee,
or maybe something hazelnut,

or something really dark and winey like Kona,
or something sludgy like the French people drink.

And when the brewing's done
does God stand out on the deck admiring the yard

wondering why some grass grows
but some doesn't?

Does he let his mind wander,
his faraway sight drifting to the left,

pulling up centuries of memory,
of all time that was then?

And then, after a few sips,
does he finally allow himself to look up to the right,

towards a blue that just matches his eyes,
and think, yes, today, I have a lot to do today?

VIGIL

One day
when I was in the nursing home
watching my father sleeping
an angel drifted through the ceiling
and stood beside me.
He put his hand on my shoulder
and he said,
"It doesn't matter
how many times
you come here to watch him.
You will never catch up.
That's how eternity works."

ALL THE PARTS OF THE BUFFALO

I contemplated a longer relationship with him until I understood
just how much he was a poet.
There we would be, enjoying a meal and conversation together
on some restaurant patio, a quiet, romantic, moment,
maybe with candles,
when someone would catch his eye,
probably another woman who had a translucent sheen to her hair,
      or a cruel set in her lips,
      or a peculiar, sensuous but oblivious turn in her ankle,
and suddenly he would be lost in scribbling something down on a napkin
or on the back of an old receipt.
For that point on any words I would say to him would bounce off his ears
to flap helplessly on the sidewalk.
I knew what was going on: before the poem was done
he would have taken that woman, chosen a view and scene,
examined her, taken her apart,
then rebuilt her, like some literary Pygmalion, all while I was sitting
there,
there, there, there in front of him.

One time I warned an unsuspecting woman what he was doing
but she couldn't understand what I was saying.
She said we were both creepy.

It is the nature of woman to have secrets;
it is the nature of poets to pry.

After the meal was cold and the poem written
he would finally return to me and apologize.
I watch everything, every little part is important, he would say.

Yes, I would say, I agree.

AT THE STONE SUPPLY YARD

Sometimes it can be a secret
    and sometimes not.

There are scores of colors and names:
    Arizona slab,
    Colorado tumble,
    Southwest rough chop.

Look here, this pieces of Limestone Coarse has a fossil in it,
    a fern,
    petite, forever, tiny fronds eternally eager for the sun.

I look at my daughter, digging through the piles of stones.
    she is intent on beauty, the perfect fit;
    I imagine beyond her

    to the mountains, the river beds, the torn hills,
    squared, hollowed and cut,
    that these stones came from
    and I wonder:

is the grass starting to grow there?
does the stream flow again?
What was a mountain is it finding peace as a plain?
Were all intrusions a secret?
Was there ever an indifference?
Did the land remember the weight that now was gone?

        A tear fell on the stone in my hand.

I felt a sudden breeze I had felt countless times before,
and thought I saw something out of the corner of my eye,
    a son, an older son, something never shared, a mistake never
    admitted.

It takes a woman to understand the bearing of that weight,
the adding by hour and day and week,
the swelling, the heft, the roundness of it.
I remembered when the foot would stick under my ribs
  and it was so firm I was sure it would leave a mark there always.

  I resolved not to decide on a name until I saw him;
    but I tried every name I knew for its sound.
  Then, one day, there was no heartbeat.
  There was the heavy silence.
    And he was taken.

  It took months to believe he was not there.
  I felt the dead weight inside, the pushing.
  The mountain became a plain;
  I was still aware of the absence.

All these stones:
so large,
so small,
so many cents per pound.

I cannot do this.
I cannot carry this another day:

  the awful weight of a
    million steps I took with empty arms,
    a thousand names I never got to call you,
    a hundred names for stone.

WHALES

The water of Khatangskiy Bay lap on the gray rocks of the estuary where the river seeps down like a low leak from a rooftop.

The source of the river is lost in the tundra somewhere north and west of the town of Novorybnaya but it is fed in other ways:

As snowmelt it dribbles gray down furtive alley-rows between the stone and slate houses, puddling momentarily outside doorways, waiting for the unwary boot, before settling lower toward the sea; as antler-shake from the caribou who stumbles into town, confused, challenging fences; as what falls black and frozen from the boots of sailors.

As part of the background music that is the wind of the arctic night and the drop of water always in the walls there is also the great sigh of the pale, beached beluga whales.

It was not something the older residents remember ever happening. No, no whales ever beached there when they were younger.

The people in town had attempted to do the noble things at first, to push the whales back into the sea; they had gathered on the shore in the dark, lanterns and lights bobbing;

They had tried to roll the whales, gray rocks sticking to the whales' ice-coated sides; the people had tried sleds and litters and skids, anything to pull the whales across the pack to any spot of open water; to the spots where the whales had burst through;
They had used ropes, many ropes, ropes tied around the whales, tied around themselves in case they fell in, all the whales having to be moved like ghostly, fat women whose husbands have left, who do not care to live, turning, eyes rolling, eyes red.

But in the end there was too much ice and too many whales and too much night.

Now the mad lovers come down to the frozen shoreline in the long night. They point to the stars on the horizon of the tanker lights heading north and east. They take long walking sticks, the sticks they use to test the strength of the ice, and they poke at the beached whales; they open the whales's mouths, disgusted by the meager krill and the gray muck that clings inside. And finally the lovers turn away, hold hands, try to hear powerful eternal voices in the gnashing of icebergs.

There is no burying of the carcasses of the whales; mottled red crabs devour them, the heaving slow gnaw of the shore ice claims what it can, children kick the bones.

AT THE AIDS CLINIC

"I should have been married by now,"
She told me, even though she was only fifteen.
The ebony skin was pulled tight around her skull,
her eyes were dry and protruding.

It was not easy for her to talk
but she needed to.
I always saved Suwana for the last stop on my rounds
there at the hospital in Liberia.

I was a smoker.
She would always poke me
in the chest and say in broken English,
"Those cigarettes—they will kill you."

We would always laugh at that, every night.
Every night when the jungle-humid air would
waft into the tents,
every night when I would make my rounds through the AIDS clinic.

I would always ask her what I could do for her.
She would always come up with something new.
"Make me twelve years old again." "Turn me into a river
so I may float away." "Tell me what movies are like."

But mostly I would just listen. I could do that.
She would tell me what her simple dreams were:
a husband who would provide, a house with stable walls,
many children, some jewelry maybe to match her smile.

"I should have been married by now,"
she told me, every night. She would shift a little in bed,
try to drink some water,
shake her head at my offer of bread or rice.

Every night, in the humidity, the last stop on my rounds,
I'd smoke a cigarette, she would chide me,
I would ask what she would need.
I would listen.

Then, one night, she said, "I think I will not
be getting married, eh?"
I took a long, smoke-filled breath and said,
"No, I do not think so."

"Then do this for me: tonight help me become invisible."
I reached and held onto her, pulled her cheek against mine.
She breathed once, smiled,
and was suddenly lighter, lighter than air.

THE ADJECTIVES OF TRUTH

When you are ten and it suddenly becomes a matter
of examining what is truth and what isn't
you realize, without being able to put words to it,
there should be adjectives of truth,
like a yellow truth, or a magenta truth,
or a gravelly truth, or a burning truth.
Half-truths and God's truth aren't explicit
or descriptive enough because they aren't really concrete.
And being concrete is everything when you are ten.

When you are ten there should be dog truths
and teacher truths and floating-stick-in-the-stream truths
and bait-that-stays-on-the-hook truths.
Instead, you are told there are absolutes,
telling a lie or telling the truth, and nothing in between,
even as your mind struggles with multiple versions of the Bible.

It gets no better as you get older. Granted,
it would be both comforting and disquieting to be driving down
a highway only to see a sign that says,
"The True Road." But ultimately wouldn't you like to know
if that road is going to be bumpy or paved?

And do we really want to know the truth, the big truth?
Isn't it the absence of truth that drives us?
Consider Thomas and the crucifixion: he actually
had to touch a true truth. Are we prepared to be
that demanding and surprised?

In the small town I grew up in there were two churches.
One was down the road from a beer hall and the other
was up on a hill. Evidently there was a high truth and a
low truth. The members of each congregation both knew
the other was going to Hell. I thought that the quarter mile of highway
between them must be Purgatory.
And maybe high and low are the two best adjectives about truth.
My wife keeps her reflexology books in a pile on the coffee table.
She has said, and I believe her, that each book is different.
Some say this spot on your hand is for the pancreas, others
say for the liver, and some say for the head. And I say to her

if reflexology is such a science then why is there such variation?
She just smiles and rubs my hand until she finds a spot that hurts.
That tells me there is a soothing-like-the-ocean truth, and a
transient truth,
and a makes-the-hurt-go-away truth and elevated truth.

That tells me that maybe it is all in the adjectives,
that maybe I should stop considering whether
something is transient or absolute,
that maybe I should just be content with the truth
that comes from the book
that is on top.

POETIC JOURNEY

Let no one pay me honor with tears, nor celebrate my funeral rites with weeping.
Ennius, 239-169 b.c.

It was a foolish agreement you and I had made
in the exuberant days of our youth,
in the days when promises were as profuse as blossoms,
when all of our words were new and each page a discovery.

I am a frayed and aging sight on this Vespa.
I am aware of that, but I am making
my slow and necessary way
down Italy, much like a migration or a seasonal river;
it needs to be done, regardless of appearance.
Tomorrow will be Pedum, birthplace of Tibullus,
the day after will be Suessa Arunca, home to Lucillus,
and, if I am diligent, on to Nepolis, source of Statius.

There were many poets in ancient Italy. Perhaps I
will make it as far back around as Mantua
(a lofty goal to end with Virgil!)

But we had sworn to each other, in words thicker than blood:
        whoever dies first then the other
            will scatter the ashes where poets have walked.

So I parse out your ashes here in Italy,
a spondee here, an iamb there, a teaspoon, a smidge,
a sooty phrase; each day I touch you for a final time,
at least once.
Today I am in Rome.
Pardon me. Something must have flown into my eye.
It is too early for Catullus but still I will say it:

it is difficult suddenly to lay aside a long-cherished love.

JESUS STOPPED BY AND FIXED MY GRILL

Jesus stopped by today
and raised my grill from the dead.
It made me question the whole
divine spark of life issue.
I started mourning for all the toasters
I might have tossed too soon.
And blenders. And piece of junk lawnmowers.
Maybe they could have been reclaimed.

I can't honestly say the parts on my grill
look new. I mean, consider
that it's not as if the people he raised from the dead
came back as babies after all.
It wasn't a do-over, a start-again at go.
And no one was made immortal.
No, it was only a pause, a deferral,
a holding off of the imperial inevitable.

My grill just works now. It's still rusty.
The shelves are loose. But it fires up.
I offered Jesus a beer in thanks,
if he had a minute,
but he smiled and declined,
said he was on his way to some
carburetor a few blocks over.
I shook his hand, turned up the flame,
tore open the franks,

just like Lazarus must have done
after all the hosannas and news-spreading
and re-tellings.
I'm betting he ran off
somewhere privately with his wife
checking to see what parts still worked.

NO SOLICITING

I am going to have a bar installed
on my front door.
You know, the long medieval kind, on a hinge,
or maybe just an old-world beam
that sits on brackets.
Of course, such a system depends on someone
always being home
to lock up after me
when I go off to work.
So maybe I should just add iron plates
to deter hewing axes, Jehovah's witnesses,
and Girl Scouts selling cookies.
The key, of course, would need to be humongous,
for sheer intimidation purposes.
I would need something much more effective
than a lock on a diary any older sister can pry.
I need to at least have a sprinkler system for a moat,
or a Chihuahua to substitute for a spike-encrusted dog.
I need a "No!" that people will believe,
something as clear and undeniable as fate,
something that will repulse even the man
who attaches pizza coupons to my door with a rubber band.
I want to have an indication so clear
that when I'm old and less able to recall
clever literary retorts to ward off unknown knocking
that my device or sign or whatever it is
could drive off even Death.
He will read the unwelcome doormat
a letter at a time with his bony finger,
realize I am really serious,
and move on to the neighbor next door
who has high cholesterol anyway.

THE HARDY-WEINBERG LAW

The Hardy-Weinberg principle states that genetic frequencies in a population remain constant from generation to generation unless outside influences are introduced. In nature these outside influences are always in effect. Therefore, the Hardy-Weinberg principle is an ideal condition that can never be achieved.

If Columbus and La Salle
had not sailed until
their sails were perfectly ironed
then today we might
be working for the Aztecs.

Some poets will not submit their poems
for public consumption
until the lines are exactly right.
Their notebooks end up
bulging with cabochons.

It's the messiness of things
that makes them perfect:
the sugar falling
from the cinnamon roll,
the ice cream melting in the cone.

Flood waters rise
and kiss against doorways.
The fire comes
down the mountain.
The wind pushes trees into yards.

When I was much younger
I wrote the characteristics
of my perfect girl
on a piece of paper,
did a little chant,

then burned the list in a coffee can,
sending my wishes to the universe.
Now you are sleeping in the crook of my arm,
and maybe you are drooling a little,
and definitely snoring,

and I am thankful for all bugs
that will ever land in my coffee,
grateful for all nails
that will ever make my tires
breathless.

TYPEFACE

This poem is set in a typeface
called Apocryphal Hominid 10 point.
Its curlicues and unexpected angles
may be confusing.
It may seem as if
you have been submerged in lines
or reduced to mere symbols.
You may begin to think too much about the presentations
and too little about what they represent.
As if when you see a beautiful woman on the street
and your mind begins to wander.
You might imagine yourself walking beside her.
You might call her Estrella
and she might call you *mi roble, mi momento*.
She will have a slightly chubby bottom,
heels half an inch too tall.
In 1611 a slightly deranged monk
had too much wine and found a way
to codify both pleasures of the flesh
and a rather horrific cataclysm in
marginal letter-endings and stylized curls.
It was a secret all about sound and image
and, especially, symbol congruency, easily
translatable once you knew the key.
Mi momento. No tree lives forever,
not even Yggdrasil. You will want Estrella
to choose what you will do, as if she will know.
You will want her to know.
She will unlatch the watch from your wrist,
and say it is all about the sounds
that will happen next.

WHEN ALEXANDER THE GREAT'S MOM HAD HIS PHOTO DONE AT SEARS

She constantly chided him.
"Don't fidget. Stand up straight.
What will the Persians think?"
She had a coupon so she wanted to try him
in as many outfits as possible.
He was always so dour, even posturing;
far too grim for a five-year old.
But he was no more grim than she was smart:
she was going to take advantage of this phase,
the tilting of his head,
the puffing of his infantile chest.
Of course, he did keep talking in the third person
and that bothered her some.
"Alexander does not like this background.
These shoes pinch Alexander's feet.
Alexander will comb his own hair."
And when the bow tie came up he simply said,
"I would not be Alexander."—and refused to put it on.
He tried the cowboy outfit, under duress,
sitting astride a wooden horse
(which still bore the 'Made in Thessaly' label—
she could have died.)
He seemed relatively comfortable--
but kept calling the conchos "girl's baubles."
When he tried on the tiny pin-stripe suit
he only quit scowling when he realized
the matching tie had a picture of Aristotle.
It was when she relented, finally,
and allowed him to stand, bare-chested,
one foot propped up on a carpeted step,
a fist clenched and close to his body,
the other arm extended like a spear,
that she dared followed his eyes
that were looking through, and past, the cameraman,
and for a chilling, pride-filled second
she believed, as only a parent can believe,
that he could crush the world
beneath those sandaled, dimpled feet.

BEFORE YOU DISAPPEAR

If you're squeamish, don't prod the beach rubble
—Sappho

you are allowed to look back once.
You always harbored the secret wish
you would be lifted at the last possible second
out of harm's way
and dropped into someone's swaddling arms.
But instead you are drifting, looking down,
bemused and detached.
You know the French have a word for it
(and you know what the word is):
the name for things that are left in a person's pocket
after they die.
While you were walking around
the objects were like little moons,
circling in and out of your gravitational sphere.
Now someone is reaching into your pockets,
digging, holding their breath, looking away,
and pulling out the pieces
that no longer have a need to orbit.
He will stir them with his gloved finger, turn them over,
catalog them. Maybe he will pat your head tenderly,
fold your hands over your chest.
This was not what you expected.
You could have worn better shoes.
Your haircut made you look old.

The only thing that matters really
is moving forward
and leaving all that debris behind.

NOT DIGESTIBLE

In the strange world of unexpected
bleak interconnectedness he was told
he could not eat peaches. Ever. It wasn't
as if they were a staple of his diet
but the doctor was very clear on the dire consequences.
He thought it would be like giving up smoking.
Suddenly peaches were on sale all over the place.
His girlfriend's shoulder was a peach.
Her left bum was a peach. The tips of her toes
were tiny little peaches. He got to the point where
he dared not speak the name of peach. There was no coping with it.
Fate had caught him using a citris lure he didn't know he wanted.
He'd have dreams of a first fuzzy bite, the nectar
running down his chin; he would nibble all the way down to the corrugated pit,
then reach into a bushel basket that was magically always full.
He'd wake up from those dreams and go to the coffee shop
and everyone there was a peach, freckled, bursting; he could
imagine little single leafs hanging from their shoulders.
He could walk in the park. There were little peach squirrels,
peach yapping dogs, the robins were colored red like ripe peaches,
little sticks of legs driving him crazy with their locomotion.
It was absurd. It was fresh fruit grimly glorious.
He found himself reminiscing like an Egyptian,
deciding how he would like to be ferried along:
In some ringed and labeled can,
caressed by heavy syrup,
intending to be sweet forever,
unreachable by wasps.

EVERY OTHER DAY

Some bones it's best
to not have gaiety over.
It's unappreciated.
They don't want to be missed.

They are still peeved about departing,
swear they can still be bruised,
are sensitive about how
light seems so direct.

En masse they appear
so unpolluted
you expect them to flesh up
and sniff toward you.

They refuse to admit it's over.
They corral up, wait for you,
tails to the wind, sure as sunlight
they'll be herded soon.

You expect dry, chitinous hooves
to clatter through your dreams,
scratchy bawls wailing
down dry arroyos.

Over there, in that copse,
may be waiting some of your relatives on horseback,
cracked saddles not squeaking,
dusty cigarettes in white fingers.

Some spirits won't queue up,
don't like you reminding them
they have a final place
they're supposed to go.

FAMOUS MOVIE STAR

The title of this poem is the name of the famous star
whose movie you have just seen recently.
See? Your eyes went and checked to make sure it was
or wasn't.
But you wanted it to be and so I wanted it to be.

And since it was about an actor
then you wanted it to be that good actor,
that muscular one maybe,
but not so muscular that it was frightening,
strong enough to lift you but only out of harm's way.
A good hero is always in harm's way.
He is always lifting someone out of harm's way.
So maybe, now you know the title,
that's what you expect in this poem,
something that will lift you out of harm's way.

You might have checked the title again just to make sure
as if something had magically changed the title
because that is what films do.
What if it was an actress, someone lithe and gracious and smart
and noble and perhaps rich,
and someone who was also good
with twelve kinds of oriental weapons?
And someone who could dance. She must be able to dance.
Man cannot always dance in movies—
But women always can. It is one of the laws of the movie universe.
So you expect this poem to be able to dance,
perhaps one two three, or a foxtrot, maybe a tango?
Did you ever realize movies had built-in meter?

So here in this movie theatre that is this book
you see the title and have expectations
because now, in the darkness,
even though there might not be darkness,
here in the darkness of the space that belongs
only to you and the title and the poem,
then you must realize that the poem belongs to you.
It doesn't matter how many other people
have seen this movie or read this tile or scanned this poem.
This time, right now, this space belongs to you.

It is your hands holding the book,
your eyes framing the words.
It is your breath fogging the air.

All of the poems you have ever read
were about you. Even Twinkle Twinkle has an I in it.
The Raven. The Grass. Innisfree.

Sooner or later
someone will make a movie about this poem.
It will lift people out of harms way.
It will make them dance.

You will be in it.

IN CASE OF POETRY READING BREAK GLASS

It is almost certain this is a scenario that will never happen.
If someone spontaneously combusts while reading something
by Bukowski then perhaps they should be allowed to burn.
Then let's all go for the axe.

Of course, the sign could read, "In case of fire break glass"
and inside the tiny little alcove,
the shelf barely big enough to hold a ancient dwarf mummy,
would be a poetry book

which most of us, I fear, would not know how to use.
We would stare blankly at it for several seconds,
wondering what possible good it could do us,
how it might yet save our lives.

LIGHT YEARS AWAY

According to the cosmology of bed
the binary suns of our heads
must be at the same level,
while the galaxies of our bodies
are stretched out.
And the little painted stars
on your toe-nails
must always be searching and stretching for,
but will never get close to,
the far-off plutoids of my feet
buried in the deep darkness
of blankets.

WHERE THE MAGIC LIES

"Her fingers know the dark corners of my mind, . . ."
—Walt McDonald, "Marriage"

When I am busy with some other thing
I have seen her leave the house,
dog on leash in one hand
and my walking stick in her other.

It isn't that her own stick isn't sturdy enough.
Teeth marks and indentations
along the grain will testify
to many a direct encounter.

But she carries my stick with her today,
sure my initials will scare anything.
She swears she can just throw it on the ground
and it will consume all serpents in her path.

And I will testify it is simply her touch
that could make any old stave feel divine,
make it burst into blossom where there
was only bark before.

SILVER AGE

The eyes, surrounded by lines, of course, are by Kubert,
as is the day-old beard. It is always a day-old beard.
Even after I shave. Sgt. Rock always had a shadow.
I always have a shadow.

You might think I have no input at all from Gil Kane
but if the light is just right
you'll see the vertical tendon
that goes from my cheekbone to the top of my jaw,
there for no apparent reason.

There's a hint, I'd like to think, from Carmine Infantino
in the little half smile I'm casting, kind of like when
Barry Allen was first starting to date Iris and couldn't let her know
he was actually The Flash.

There, at the base of my neck, you might notice the
lax skin, wrinkled, kind of turtle-like, freckled.
Why do I look so stretched out right there, you might say
and then you will realize that
Berni Wrightson was given the shoulders and neck
and he really likes to add a touch of pending macabre,
full of sinew and age.

My bushy eyebrows are obviously Barry Smith
in his finest Zukala-Conan period. It is a shame
that I cannot conjure demons.

My head is long. Jim Aparo did that.
He's always liked long heads. That—and he drew
the little silver in my hair around my temples
like on The Phantom Stranger.

You notice how I am facing the mirror squarely,
emphasizing the shoulders. You can even see the
lines of my breastbone through the t-shirt.
That's because Jack Kirby drew that part of me that way
(although there are times I think someone else
might have done the inking.)

Sadly, there is no part of me that is Steranko,
No false perspectives, no layering of muscles.
And neither is there any part of me that you can see
that is penciled, and penciled only, by Neal Adams.
I stay within the frame. I am not cinematic.

And lastly,
if the mirror was only a little wider
then you would see just off to the side
my concubine, obviously designed by Wally Wood,
her massive bosom perfectly round,
and impossibly full.

THE VERITABLE SPEED OF LIGHT

If all time is now
then I do not feel too guilty
about dropping everything else
that I should be doing
and instead writing down
this poem that is
speeding through my brain.
This is one of those
express trains of a poem
that has come barreling unscheduled
from some far-off city of inspiration
and doesn't intend to stop
so I'll just have to try and snag
what sounds and images I can.
The trashcan sits un-emptied
by my chair and bunnies graze
in the grass I should mow.
But all time is now I tell myself again,
as if that will stop everything.
Vesuvius will still need to grumble
but not yet smother Pompeii,
the Spartans will still hold Thermopylae,
the Mayans will still be running around
chipping calendars from stone,
and the tiny little chain
of Caribbean islands
whose name I always forget
will not yet be swallowed
by the sea.

DIRECT ADDRESS

In a road movie
I especially liked the way
Bob Hope would turn right to the fourth wall
and speak to the audience.
Sometimes he would warn us
that Bing Crosby was about to sing.

As far as I know there is no version of the Bible
where suddenly there's a section,
probably italicized,
where Jesus would speak to you directly.
"Bob, don't take that job."
"Denice, stick to the salad."
Then he would return to the action,
trying to coach the thick disciples.

That's why we think poetry has no pertinence.
There's no Whitman talking about grass,
Farnsworth moaning about dragons,
Browning making us an accomplice in regards to a Duchess,
or Dickinson whispering to us about death.

And certainly nothing is calling us by name.
Not even Robert Frost. Or Sandburg.
Who's out there now, offering us a hand?

Sure, there's Thomas, telling us not to go gentle.
But he's dead.

What I want to know is:
Who is out there, right now,
offering me a contract I want to sign,

writing lines that linger and resonate,
something lyrical and sympathetic,
poems that are smart, with some clever dialogue,
with the added ingredient of something equivalent
to a smiling Dorothy Lamour.

IN THE LAP OF EDDIE THE GIANT

He comes slowly when called.
We hear him groan in the cave of his room.
He bends to come through the doorway,
impossible hands on the frame two feet above the knob.
He pulls himself through, rising.
He breathes large like a tunnel.

He sits slowly down in his chair,
knees as high as our heads.
One by one, up and down, he lifts us.

His arms are beams, his legs logs.
We can only see the shafts of his nostrils.
We have no words big enough to talk.
It is like climbing on a statue.
Or telling a Christmas list to Frankenstein.

Our parents take pictures, pay Eddie's father.
Without saying a word Eddie goes back to his room,
his hands drooping like tired shovels.

With our courage restored us boys go outside,
square our shoulders, say what we have done,
remark how big we have become.

ON THE SHORES OF LESBOS

A shepherd who myth has not named
found Orpheus's head (after the Maenads
had torn him apart.) The dead tongue still seemed to sing
although the eyes were quiet in their doom.

So that poor shepherd of Lesbos carried
the head into his home. Wonder
of wonders! A head that sang still!
What gift was this? What things might yet change?

Might the goats give more milk,
the sheep give up more wool?
Might the wolves shadowing the hillsides
be made more wary by the music?

But the Gods had long since abandoned
those lips. The singing was only
the wind's memory. That shepherd
of Lesbos had only a guttural head

sitting there, its muscles and jaws in final
atonal grindings of power. It could barely make
a broom shiver in a corner.
The sheep bleated plaintively—once.

PREREQUISITE

Let None But Geometers Enter Here
—motto inscribed above the door at Plato's Academy
where the principal studies were forms and the universe.
4th Century—just outside of Athens.

One would assume you needed to show up
with your own measuring rope.

Or at the very least some pre-defined rod
that was exactly the length from elbow to fingertips.

And a bag-full of pre-conceived notions.
Back then there seemed to be no shortage of pre-conceived notions.

Evidently, they wrote endlessly about the stars—
but never went outside to actually study them.

What is the sense of that?
But that's a foolish question

as I sit here, now, in this incredibly uncomfortable chair,
in this equivalent of a suburban, informal academy,

listening to open-mic poets
reading their own poetic philosophies

and it is obvious they have never stepped outside
themselves to see other constellations.

There should have been a sign
over the doorway over the bookstore.

These poets have not yet learned how to measure.
They should have brought their own rope.

SELF-DETERMINATION

This morning I think I will choose creamer in my coffee
as opposed to jumping my fence and crossing the border
into the Horrible Land of Prickle Wigglies.

If only all mornings had choices this simple.

There was yesterday. It was also easy.
I was driving.
I had to choose between turning left into the tacqueria
or right into the Pass of the Zombie Kings.

But last week, at a soiree,
I had to choose between cucumber sandwiches
or confronting a fearsomely attractive and well-armed cadre
of Amazonian women.
I debated that one.

A person shouldn't have to anguish over
each and every second.
This minute, that moment, this route, that route,
little swallow, big swallow, one pill, two pills.
Even that first ambitious lungfish had to primally choose
between swimming away
or painfully walking, however briefly, up a dry slope.

It can feel benign at the time:
choosing between Lou Ann Smurnick
or Debbie Zombalo to take to the prom.
But there are always ripples
and you can't always see downstream.

Like Archimedes who could have left
his unfinished design in the dust
but instead chose to ask the Roman soldier
to kindly step out of the light.

WHAT I DO NOT EAT

These are not apples from the sun.
These are not apples from the moon.
This bowl of fruit is simply fruit,
and here is more than yet enough

of space beside me on the bench.
And here's a glass, a fork, a plate. And what
I do not eat I may
discard, so no birds echo songs

of gaping mouths, just there and there,
that sing their thin and burbly scales.
If I dare bite the dappled skin,
if my lips touch the cooling glass

what might be said to make me think
of palms outstretched, of bowing heads,
the thin, webbed hands, and boney cheeks,
and tongues that know a thousand woes.

What I do not eat at night
I do not think about at all.
It simply sits, like unstirred sin.
The doors are locked, I dim the lights.

In far-off days I might have heard
some poems that might have fed us all.
But they were selkies. I forgot.
They passed into the myth of night.

SOUTHWEST

MR. SANCHEZ

Mr. Sanchez, lean and dry and old,
assailed by ague, bright with morning fever,
still had the strength when morning dew was falling
to swim the muddy waves of Galveston Bay.

At first his arms were hesitant in the water.
(He'd left his wife asleep beside him in the bed;
he'd crept softly in his socks and sweat-soaked long johns
to quickly don some trunks, then to the beach.)

But then the ocean (ah, that saltine hissing,
his burning skin caressed by tiny snails
and kelp, the insistent butting of nibbling fish)
reached out and gave him confidence.

He knew his lungs were full of pneumonia,
had been for days. He was making no progress
against the foul thing (or so he thought of it—
he'd fought too hard too long to be laid low.)

He had not swam for weeks and lying there
only a shell beneath the sheets and quilts
he knew that after seventy years of swimming the bay
he'd drown, ironically, in bed.

He knew that as a bitter fact until last night
when, his lungs near full and rest so very near,
he felt a vigor come into his arms
and saw a gentle light behind his eyes.

His skin is cooler now, his fever broken.
he faintly heard the sound of parting tears.
he raised his head just once from out the water
then crossed the bar with strong and guided strokes.

A PAINTING OF A BLACKSMITH

The right arm drawn back and over his head,
the left holding the tongs that bite
the metal rod, the fire-tinged thing,
waiting for the strike.

The focus of the eyes,
the set of the bicep,
the flat stance of the legs
and the solid, immutable grip of desire.

There should be a word
for the imagining of an echo,
for when that hammer hits,
when the need for shape is sent through an arm,

for when the hammer calls
and the hot metal answers,
and the clang and shimmers
go through the anvil into the boots.

This is the painting I want you
to dream of me at night:
the breathless gasp right before
the arm swings around,

the knowing that you need only touch me
and I will be hungry with fire,
that you need only call me
and I will ring red and sparking and true.

AT MIZ HESTER'S SOCIAL HOUSE

Before she would let us be led upstairs
she would make us sit in the parlour
and listen to her reading from the Bible,
at least ten verses.

We'd rather string fence
or milk reluctant cattle.
We never realized how much
begatting could weigh on a man.

But sitting there with God on one hand
and the willing flesh on the other,
with our worn hats nervous in our laps
and our thin boots digging in the rugs

we didn't have the heart,
or the settled state of mind, to tell her
we were already way past saving,
souls and all.

FENCE DUTY ON THE LAZY L

When the land had been firm
we had strung wire on those posts.

Now, during the drought,
our eyes could follow the lines of split soil.
Odd, we would say, how the ground would separate
in circles at first around the posts, like stacked rings,
and then start fingering off, large running cracks,
tiny earthquake faults.

We would scour for rocks and jam them down the holes,
make the posts upright, make the fence lie about
its strength.

Where there had been grass there was a memory,
along with any moisture. An overflowing well
was a dream. One man said even his wife's lips were dry.
My eyes opened more scratchy every day. All of our dogs
would bark raspy.

And every day that fence continued to fall, the ground continued
to craze. The earth would swallow the rocks;
we'd have to find more. Each day, driving up, we would see those fence
posts tilting like falling flags, poles we had righted
just yesterday.

So we would walk out through the dust, again,
pulling and jabbing and jamming,
thinking that in the pattern of the tilting posts,
in the writing of the mud hieroglyphs,
there had to be a message if we could only read it,
or had enough faith.

Maybe if we could follow the perfect peeling track with our feet,
     or undo the correct twisted line with our eyes,
          then it might lead us to a bubbling well
          or the sky might reward us, yes.

But it didn't, and still we kept coming back, it was our job,
and everyday was the tilt then the pull,
     and the rocks so hot we could barely hold them
before we threw them into the maw of the earth.
There was no answer in those baked pathways,
     no way out for our blind steaming faith.

It was a knot we couldn't untangle,
     a path without a clue,
     a dry labyrinth we couldn't escape.

RIGHT BEFORE YOU LEAVE EL PASO

going east there ought to be a kind of customs stop
where you are instructed to call to mind
all the songs you know
and sing them right into something sturdy.

Imagine that place:
"Here, Bobby, here's a candy wrapper, and, Sue, here's
a little extra room in a suitcase. Dad can have all the empty pop bottles
because he knows a lot of songs."
(And some folks, the ones who are poor and aren't toting much,
will be convinced to hum right into a paper bag,
or up their shirt sleeve, or into a shoe.)

Imagine a Ranger grabbing Grandma by the ankles,
shaking all the tunes loose.
"We'd better not hear you singing out loud
until you at least hit Alpine.
We can't take your radios
but we'll be listening if you sing along…"

Heading back south and east into the Rio Grande
the Big Bend doesn't tolerate much talking.
It's too big a place, too set in silence,
and all the people who have been here before have tried to fill it up.

But the Rangers say they can't tolerate any more nights
where the hot, humid wind carries pieces of old, foolish, brave voices
and impales them on the claws of the ocotillo and lechuguilla,
leaving torn shreds of songs
that weep and shriek and drift
from cactus to mesquite, from bush to thorny bush.

SIGNS

If we'd listened we might have heard
some dread crows warning us.
If we hadn't been so full of sleep we might have seen
the sun come up behind black and green clouds.

Our horses, somehow, saw it coming first,
and tried to steer us home but too late then!
A slate-gray sky came down
and exploded on us with a sudden rush.

We closed our mouths and bent our heads
but that wind turned each seam and hidden fold.
Our boots turned into buckets.
Our brims fell flat against our eyes.

So we decided: we breathed once, deep,
then yee-hawed it, yipped and roared,
threw our heads back, foolish, daring,
slapped the reins, and cheered our horses to lather, set for home,

and laughed at all Fates that would drown us,
and washed ourselves with sopping bravado,
our horses' prints washing away in the mud
even as they were stamped.

We were cavalry leading a hopeless charge,
fearless of the spears of rain, the missiles of hail,
laughing and cursing that we hadn't scried the thunder,
but still looking up to read the twisting entrails of the sky.

WHAT MAKES IT STOP

It is a fact that the beer companies wait at least
five years to ship calendars to rural beer halls.
It's like a mix between an Almanac and a Bible.
It's comforting to know what the days were just a few years ago.

There was only ever one picture; the months
were stapled on below, but they never advanced
much past April, maybe May (depending on when the
month-turner had realized it just didn't make much difference.)

One or two calendars had Jesus in some holy pose,
a few had tractors with some of the cleanest, happiest
farmers ever, but the most reliable were the calendars
with women captured in mid-sip and red-lip smile.

Her toe always pointing at Saturday, her red/blonde/brunette
curls thrown back (the hair color was truly both crucial
and unimportant) she'd be holding a bottle of soda with one hand
and her other arm would be hardly covering her bare breasts.

That calendar was always hanging on the wall behind
the beer cooler, as if rendered invisible unless
you were drinking a grown-up drink.
The connection of Sin was not lost on me.

But the wisdom of handy electrical sockets
had placed the soda cooler next to the beer.
In the middle of Summer (or March according to the calendar)
I could reach down into the cold water and grab Winter

or at least late Autumn. My fist full of dripping
Nehi, RC, or Coke, every time I would try to see
if that calendar had changed but I could never
remember from visit to visit, distracted by that picture.

"Don't look," my father would say, struggling to avert
his own eye from all that leg and cleavage.
But it was hopeless. We found ourselves taking
long sips in place as time stood still.

Even now I remember looking at that calendar and thinking
she must have been beautiful back then,
back when Thursday fell on a Monday,
back when my birthday was on a day I couldn't seem to recall.

THE RED HAND AT KABAH

Margarita Angelina Alfonso would say
that the red hand painted
on the arch at Kabah was actually painted
by one of her ancestors,

and that another one of her ancestors
painted the matching blue hand
on the other arch at Uxmal
at the end of the sacbe
that joined the two cities.

And she knew this, she would tell us,
because she had Mayan blood
in her veins.

It took skill to climb so high,
without rope or ladder,
to paint the colored hands she would say.
But then everyone would see—
and they would take that journey knowing
there was an ending and a beginning.

And who's to say it wasn't true?

We did know that her husband
was the most handsome man
any of us had ever seen.
He would sometimes stick feathers in her hair
and make her blush.

We also knew that when they danced together
they always knew the edge of the dance floor.
Their nostrils always flared together.
Their feet always knew exactly
when the music would stop.

MESQUITE

They always
look older than they are
as if they are aged and bent
by each big blow.
Then afterwards
they send out
a new line of green spokes
in toothy resentment
for not being stronger-willed.
Yet their grip
on the earth
is iron.
They're not leaving,
not surrendering
an inch of dirt,
steadfast patriots
to their plot.
Thinking of using the wood
for that special smoke?
Best you leave
your axe at home.
There's a thought
that says they talk
across county lines.
Word gets out
of your hewing nature
you might find
an unexpected tine
through a Sunday shoe.
Best in this drought-land
to pull up a catawampus
but sturdy stool
and lean against the furrowed bark
to enjoy the thin shade.

Best you can do to listen
to the whispering click-clack
of the bean pods
fixing to fall,
the tiny, tangy gifts
the tree will give you
if you just ask,
like an undeserving supplicant
hungry for a
mealy manna.

THE COUSIN WHO SAW THE UFO

pulled his story inside him
like a religion he had abandoned.

He told the story once,
let others pass it on,
finally denied it.

He grew circles under his eyes
like old potatoes, thick and puffy.
Sometimes he would get up in the middle of the night
and start and stop and start his car.

There was a tiny fear inside him now—
like buying a seedpack
at the hardware stone
waiting for geraniums
and something brown, ragged and musky coming up.

It was something that could fill a person
unexpectedly,
like when you were little,
staying up past the lightning bugs,
barefooted, in the yard,
the stars suddenly too deep,
your father's hand too far away.

It was like almost being asleep, your eyes shut,
seeing ghostly strings floating in your eyes,
and hearing muffled, against your pillow,
what might be your heartbeat
or not.

THUNDERSTORM OUTSIDE OF LAMESA

On that treeless plain
the storms can come out of nowhere,
big, black things that
chew up the horizon in minutes.

You don't stand outside
to thank God for rain.
The raindrops are full of grit.
the lightning is fickle.

But the ghost that stands watch
in the small old cemetery
at the edge of the yard
never leaves her spot.

She ignores the hailstones
that fall through her.
She doesn't wipe her forehead
or pull back sopping hair.

She looks at me and points west
always trying to remind me
the hot, dry wind will be back,
reclaiming what it owns.

RAISING DUST ON CADDO PEAK

"When it doesn't rain, we water,
pumping the purest water three hundred feet
straight up from nothing we've ever seen…"
　　　　From "Making Book on the Aquifer", Walt McDonald

In this drought geologists say we can't drill deep enough.
There's cactus then rock,
then shale, then rock,
then nothing.

It's hard to imagine
one day fish swam here,
but I can stir up fossils with my boot;
it's mute evidence enough.

Witching's a wasted art;
might as well let the hazel gather dust.
Cows wander off their paths,
their noses not leading them in any direction.

Snakes don't bother pushing venom,
baby's feet are safe from scorpions that don't strike.
Raccoons give up washing.
Acorns break down, dry as chaff.

There's no squint sharp enough
to see clouds past the horizon,
not even up here on this forgotten tower,
not even this close to God's unweeping eye.

EVENT, CLARITY

In Lubbock, in the middle of summer nights,
when the power would go out and the fans would die on us,
then we would remember the cast iron bed
had wheels, so we would creakily negotiate it

out the door and across the yard
and park it there in clear view of the road,
and you'd wear something flannel
and I'd wear faded boxers,

and you'd lay your head on my chest.
The moon was an icebox cooling our eyes and cheeks;
it was white and pocked like a thin,
late winter Texas snow,

and we would watch satellites
drift overhead like determined fireflies,
watch them blink steady like breaths we had to take,
like our heartbeats measuring the length of night.

WHEN TOMMY LEFT

It sure was a big deal when Tommy left.
He was the only son, grew up horsey-thick and iron-strong.
"He's good. He's a damn good boy!"
Someone slapped Daddy on the back, big, sweeping, painful whacks.

That war was fifty years ago but I know I should have told Tommy,
I should have told him, but I was twelve, I didn't have the words.
And besides, I didn't know at first, not at dinner outside there
by the comforting church canopied by the God-blessed red oak
and dropping pecan, surrounded by the town.

The congregation supplied the vegetables, Daddy the meat.
Grandma was slow serving and shaky but the turkey never slipped
off the family platter ("It was grandma's grandma's.")
We held our breath, released it when we heard the platter land.

It sure was a big deal. Local boys played guitars and accordions.
I danced with Tommy twice
but he really was more for other folks than family that day.
I reached up and stroked the ridges of beginning beard on his face.

We made him take a quilt.
I tried counting the patches with my hand, eyes closed,
mouthing the numbers but I couldn't do it.
I tried again and again but I always missed some.
The mothball smell hung thick in my nose like old dead flowers.

It was when I saw he was sitting, shaking hands with old folks
that he'd known forever,
and talking quietly with Daddy,
and I was told to roll up my sleeves girl
and dive into the soap like the real women that I found out.
They let me clean the family platter because I was young and careful.

I was washing and laughing and brushing my hair back
just like Momma
when I knew.
I shivered but was silent
because as I was running my finger along the rim of the platter
I was startled by a glaze crack.
My finger halted on an unanticipated, running,
hollow-sounding crack.
I held the platter with both hands, stared at it, too aware,
rinsed it, dried it with cautious dignity,
knowing I had an audience,
then solemnly handed it back to Grandma, without a word.

We made him stand up on the table and say a few words.
Every little noise got clapping, every little burp a loud guffaw.
Later, right before he left, we made him do it again.
I should have said something then.

But I think he knew, he already knew,
when we cheerfully threw his bag
into the maw of that bus luggage compartment
and Tommy looked directly at me through a window
and his face was already pale
and I looked at the driver and could only see
eyes dark beneath a green felt brim
and a rickety smile, teeth gleaming and boney…

A LITTLE LONGER THAN THE MOMENT

Dang. I left my camera in my other shirt
I say to myself like a tourist.
Wire-cutters I brought, a hammer,
a shovel, an iron bar,
and a coffee can full of nails I'd salvaged.
An extra pair of gloves. Water.
But a camera hadn't made the list for months.

Not like there wasn't room in the truck.
Plenty of space even for some pencils,
a lined pad or old faded receipts that could
still take a mark. I could have written something down.

Why, not even two weeks ago I saw the biggest snake
I'd ever encountered coiled up and around a post,
his head as pitted and gravelly as old adobe
resting flat on top, impassive as a mummy.

That would have been a picture. Or at least a good poem.
I've seen hawks fight to exhaustion over rabbits.
I've felt the wind blowing so hard
it embedded mesquite tines like bullets in the side of the truck.
I should have taken a picture of that.

I should have taken a picture of how many nails
a post can hold. Maybe I should have written about
how when the fence wire is tight enough it sings
a real low note. A good fence has to be at least that tight.

I'm sure I have a camera somewhere. Maybe tomorrow
I will at least put a pencil and a notepad in the truck.
I have left enough blood and sweat on this landscape.
I am no longer a tourist.

THE BORDER BLASTER

On my father's route from Uvalde to Alpine
I was lying flat on the back seat of his 1958 Ford Fairlane.
Jesus promised to save me in a language I couldn't understand.

My father would turn the radio way down at night so I could sleep
but he would lay the top of the car down so I could look out.
On some nights, like tonight, it seemed as if
the stars were shrugging and shedding their patina of dust;

the sky was milky with blessing, spread out and glistening.
I remember my father would say, "Only English when we get there.
You have been here before. You know how to act."
I knew when we finally stopped in the morning
the teeth of his comb would catch in my wind-tangled hair.

We would drive through the night sometimes, like tonight,
the dot on the radio dial a little beacon.
There was only one station on the radio,
Jesus shouting he would save us, in Spanish, only Spanish.
We had a trunk full of shoes and boots and belts
and brochures, lots of brochures, all of them in English.

At night, driving, my father's brown hands would turn black,
He was a shadow at the wheel. I was a smaller shadow in the back.
I sat up in the seat, let the wind blow the Mexican words out of my head
so I would know what to say when I got to Alpine.

Pelo. Tonight I would let that word go, let it tangle
in the mesquite our car was rushing by. I decided tomorrow
I would lose *baile*. I closed my eyes, sorting words like star dust,
while Jesus promised to bless us in a language I couldn't understand.

THE LIMESTONE PIT NEAR ROUND ROCK, THE 1960'S

You could always see the cloud
during the day, there, off the freeway,
to the west, heading toward Austin.

White lime hanging like a curtain,
invisible trucks and bulldozers
behind it, roaring, hauling, chewing dirt.

Dust all the way to the freeway,
coating the median like warm snow.
If you felt the inclination

you could stop your car on the shoulder
and brush your hands on the grass,
swirl and make tiny white tornadoes.

Residents were always thankful
for the prevailing winds,
blowing the dust either north or south.

But the local church wasn't spared;
it got constantly christened with a granular manna.
The offering plate always needed turned.

I used to wonder what it would be like
to work all day and then go home
coated with lime dust.

Would the dog ever stop barking
at the daily apparition at the door?
Would I have to shake

every day outside before I could come in?
Would the wife have used up all her tsks
years ago, forget to say how lime bleached everything?

Would I finally go to bed, skin permanently pale as the sheets?
Would the friction of my body wear holes in the blankets?
Would I sigh shallow and gritty, breath like fog?

PIKAIA

He'd found the limestone slab,
a hundred pounds or more,
and brought it home. It was bristling
with fossil shells, spirals and ridges,
and strange finned things that I figured
even some scientists might have trouble naming.

I noted how the Johnson grass had advanced on the drive
and the railroad tracks were rusty from lack of use.

He was all excited and rolling that fossil thing this way and that.
I dried my hands on the dish towel I had used a thousand time before.

The cast iron skillet I was intimate with soaked in the sink.

There was a snail climbing the wall of the carport,
its pseudopod leaving a trail, the fading glistening
telling about days of work. It was 9:10 a.m.;
the mail truck was pulling up.

He was still talking;
I could see his smile without opening my eyes,
could see his smile in a knot of wood, teeth of a saw,
in the tree lined bowl of our horizon. I could smell him,
Old Spice and sweat and coffee, that's what the walls smelled like,
what the dish towel smelled like.

I could smell the sweet silk
insides of a coffin from somewhere, the wind blew it to me,
and it smelled like him too.

I bent down and admired the fossil.
There was a reflection in the replaced quartz.
It was me here, and me here, and me here.

(Pikaia: an ancient worm-like creature that may have been the ancestor to all
fishes, especially the lobe-finned fishes some of which left the prehistoric seas to
live on land. According to evolutionary theory, some of these lobe-finned fishes
changed into vertebrates and finally evolved into humans.)

PRECISE QUATRAINS AS COMPARED TO THE TEXAS PRISON RODEO

Rilke might have understood
but I doubt as it would have
gone the other way.

The gray stripes were not subtle,
and grizzled and ornery were almost certainly
not words that had connotations
anywhere close to luxurious.

Still, there was that count of eight
and that temporary feeling
that for a few hours there was
something beyond a measured space,

that something as beautifully mysterious as desire
was sitting right there
(even if it was far removed
on the other side of a dust-filled arena).

Perhaps Rilke would have
dusted himself with a silk bandana,
would have started a count to eight again,
and again, and again,
and scratched something about leaping and flying.

There would have been nothing metaphoric
about how the convicts would
have assessed him,
the small man with the pencil moustache.

But they would have understood him
a lot better once they'd heard him speak
about how things change,
about the way their sweat glistened like stars,

about how wishes were sent to heaven
with each cloud of dust,
about how there was a heady taste of freedom
every time that chute burst open wide.

CENTRUROIDES VITTATUS

There's no retreat there. He's born self–aware
and legendary, swords in hand,
dagger for a tail. He patrols
at night; best to leave him alone. Don't disturb
him, don't threaten his guarding of the mundane.
He must be of a mad god's bloodline.
Maybe he's Hector, filling the darkness of shoe
tips or skulking on the bottom of boxes.

Even when doom is certain you won't see
fear cloud his helmeted face, no sweat upon
his bronze armor. He understands how
the Gods pump the ichor of history. He's ready
to die, poisoned by courage, crushed and dragged,
still cursing and stabbing, with his final, waning breath.

(Texas striped scorpion)

THE RATTLESNAKE HUNT

"Even our beer was cold and sweeter than most and steel spoons melted in our mouths."
From "The Night of Rattlesnake Chili" by Walt McDonald

One grainy old photograph of rattlesnakes
hanging head down from the windmill
and you'd swear we lived on the frontier,
men used to clearing trees and defying cactus,
digging into sod hills.

I had never met that man inside my father
who took down his shotgun,
walked out into a limestone and mesquite field,
turned stones, and poked down holes with a hoe handle,
daring the snakes to come out.

He was a Beowulf before I knew the name.
He could have come back with just the leg
of a jackrabbit and I'd have been just as impressed.
But he returned with old brown pill bottles
full of cut-off rattles, trophies he'd claimed.

You can't see it in the photograph:
the red on his shoes, the flush in his cheeks,
the char on his knife from where he'd burned off the venom.
It was all there, you can imagine it,
call up all prairie pioneers.

You'll have to depend on me telling you that after that photo
he came in and sat that pill bottle on the kitchen table
and he reached for my Mom
and he kissed her longer than long
and he swore by God how her lips never tasted quite so good.

WHEN THE BIG RAINS CAME

Once upon a time rainwater eroded the supports
of a concrete bridge that stood twenty feet above the water.
One whole section fell in, leaving a black, unmarked gap.
I wish this was the way an adventure began, a whole story:
Oh, look, there is a man driving his old truck
in the darkness along that road. No, there is road there,
his mind insists, but really he is falling.
He will have time to roll a window down and say "Hey?"
(Few people ever get that moment of suspension.)
In a breath the man will be floating down-river in his
fendered boat, for miles, maybe hours. He will finally
run aground on some exotic shore. And there he will meet a
princess who had been waiting, who had been
watching the dark, mysterious waters roll by.

OKLAHOMA STORM

Emily Redfox scraped another sprig of sickly thistle
out from under the tomato-vine canopy,
then dug once more, slightly deeper,
to check for tenacious root.

She'd been reckoning by red-dust rivulets all day:
the sheening sweat beading waxy, speckled, pregnant,
bursting finally, swathing runes
through the dust on her arms, splashing her boots.

The moistness cooled, kept water on those internal slabs
of stone that, in turn, capped slathering lava
boiled from vials of demeaning tasks,
good-for-nothing-spouses, spoiled blood, white man's wishes.

Closer, she thought, closer still. Ah, there!
Another weed plucked by fickle, fateful blade.
Her hoe hissed on, kissed and scraped by tomato-vine whiskers.
Mrs. Birnbaum watched through shaded screen.

A breeze touched Emily's shoulder, chilled her arm,
kind of teased her lean leg, ran a wide hand down the tomatoes.
It was the only time since noon that Emily'd dared bend up.
She got paid by the plot, not the hour.

Through chain link, just in sight, Emily could see her plywood shack
sentineled by a cloud bigger'n'blacker than any mythic nigger:
a cyclone starting to descend—indiscriminate, lethal, on track.
Mrs. Birnbaum watched through shaded screen.

Emily thought: I should drop the hoe, jump the fence, grow wings,
get to the shack, pry the beer can out of his hand,
break his stupor, dodge his fists, close my ears,
drag him out the door, down the steps. Her arm wavered.

She thought again, felt the wind. Closer, closer still.
Too close now to beat the jaws.
Far enough away to miss the rip and tear.
A shadow filled the trailer's doorway.

A roaring filled her ears. She felt plates shift, exposed magma harden.
She surveyed the unhoed area, plotted a path, measured distances, costs.
She set her hands, her eyes, her lips, bent over.
Mrs. Birnbaum watched through shaded screen.

CORONADO POINTS

In Floyd County, near Floydada,
the man who lived in a nursing home
kept the chain link glove he had found over thirty years ago
in a box.

While probably important he'd been told,
it didn't prove much of anything. It had less
conversational magnetism than a box of someone else's medals.
It was just something limp lying around.

It wasn't until folks starting finding
copper crossbow points in that same canyon
where the old man had wandered
that someone who knew someone

dropped off a letter to an anthropologist
who right off said, "Coronado. Yes, I'd bet,
by God, he passed this way for that place,
look for Quivira,

where there were huge boats and monstrous fish
and 'las plata de oro.'" That anthropologist,
when he heard, had to wipe his mouth.
"You wait," he said,

"People will be digging there for years,
looking for more proof, looking for the trail."
A scanning hawk, that far-off day,
might have seen the falling glove's glimmer,

or maybe he flew on, intent on prey in
the next canyon, or maybe that glove fell
across the path of a route-ruled rattler
who, envious, of the fine scales, struck,

and then followed his natural track. Or maybe
someone should hurry back to that nursing home
in Floyd County, near Floydada, and find
that man who's still got the box,
and ask him quick, before he dies,

"Tell me,
when you first saw it lying there,
exactly which way
were the fingers pointing?"

WHEN WE BROUGHT THE TREE LIMBS DOWN

It was nothing more than a burning reflex
of muscle and bone and dare-you-to-climb-higher.
Mother had said her hydrangeas weren't getting
any sun and what could we boys do about it?

We were fools, trying to saw, and swing,
and lift more than we should. We were
sharp axes and imbalanced ladders and
watch-out's and weight on dead branches.

But finally, it was us on the ground,
sawn branches, and all boys, safe and sound.
We said oh and ah and feel that sun
and my, won't those hydrangeas grow now?

We pounded each other on the back,
stretched imaginary suspenders, said good job.
Mother cooked a huge supper.
We went to bed full of food, bravado, and sawdust.

And did not sleep. A wind came through
that night. It curled over the absent limbs
like a lost tooth. It wondered. It searched.
It sang a mournful song we did not want to hear.

SUPERMAN, FLYING OVER TEXAS,

was dubious
but Lois had said, "No. Really."
So, just after the day slid down
below the horizon
he touched a quiet red boot down
at the edge of a crowd
that had gathered at concrete tables
at a roadside park
outside Marfa.
And he was both delighted and
disconcerted
when the crowd
ignored him
because they were too wrapped up
in a glowing mystery
that was deeper and sweeter and more ooh-ah
than a perfect alien leg that could leap canyons,
a glistening forelock that would never fall.

FROM THE SPRING

There is no cenote here this morning
although I do wish there was.
This early all I want sometime is something cool
in which to immerse myself,

something so unbearably cool
that it would startle my belly and give me a clarity
so thorough I could see the stones on the bottom
as if I had newly strong vision.

At night I sometimes get this
when I take a walk later than I normally would,
and I realize that there are seams in time
when yes, the world does change

and unfold itself, and there are threads
and patterns that reassert,
and I am a part of the new pattern,
and it makes everything glisten newly minted

even in the darkness,
the well bubbling up from underneath things
touching my floating heels
as I float, float, letting things shine.

BEING KISSED UNDER THE WINDMILL

He had held onto the frame with one hand,
and clinged me up beside the ladder
till I could feel the cold welds
through my cotton dress.

I ran my fingers into his hair
and pulled his head close,
stopped him an inch away,
then crushed his lips with a rush that made him breathe.

So this was desire then,
following an invitation and nod
to drift from the vestiges
of the barbecue at night.

I opened my eyes once
and looked at him close up,
his closed eyes quivering, his nose flaring,
his cheek not a finger away.

I tilted my head back,
moaned with full intent,
and while he kissed my neck
I grabbed a support and let my weight drift back,

and I looked up inside the windmill,
up inside the receding frame of the windmill,
and I counted the frames,
I counted the layers and steps,

and, once more, I moaned,
but it was actually the moon
that had caught my attention,
it was so full, so full of pride.

I noticed that the wind suddenly changed
and hit the fin and spun the blades,
which started a tremor that ran the length of the supports,
through my arm, vibrated down into my shoes.

CLEARING CACTUS

It was a summer job: clearing cactus
off a remote section of a ranch,
a little south and west of Dalhart.

The land was too flat here, scrub stuff,
mesquite and loose limestone,
with random granite too far south.

It was tough work, long axes and thick gloves,
and a flat bed with sides
driven by a teenager too young for a license.

It wasn't like the cactus was too sinewy,
but no gloves were thick enough
and sleeves were too much in that open heat.

And besides, there was no end to the cactus;
it was a hydra: with each death,
seven more sprang up around.

It was something that got in your head:
dreams filled up with sweat and thorn and pear,
and a flat green that went on forever.

STRANGE MATTER

I envy the farmer
who, upon checking his pasture
after the tornado had torn through,
had found, of all things,
a cancelled check stuck on a barb-wire tine
that had been drawn on a bank
some three states away.
Then, without even thinking about it,
that farmer up and sent the check back
to the lady whose house it had been rudely sucked from
who promptly responded with a polite,
"Thank you for returning my property,"
and that closed the matter to all appearances,
as quirky as the facts were.

But I bet that particulate hung on a wire hook inside
that farmer's mind long after
he dropped the real item in the mail.
Why, some nights don't you just know that
his mind was up in a gray vortex,
full of wonder and spark,
sending signals to his feet to up, up, get up,
and see what else is waiting for us
out there on the edges of the
pedantic furrows,
the common loam.

WITCHING

Upon what meat doth this our Caesar feed that he is grown so great?
Julius Caesar I, ii, 148

It's hard to compete on the same water table.
I can't depend on surveyors
or the drain of an empty well.

I can hear my neighbor's pump working all night,
sucking the water up,
his irrigating wheels spraying prosperity on each boll.

Sometimes, my old equipment brings water up steady;
more often it's a trickle, rusty, a teasing of the pipes,
leaving sediment in the bottom of the water drum.

I need to go down deeper or find another hole
but the witching rod hangs unused,
unsure of its ability.

It's hard to tie envy to thirst; it's more wondering about skill.
Which row did I not plow right?
What type of seed did I not use?
Whose hand did I not shake?

His lights stay on later at night
than mine. Sometimes music travels to me.
A woman's throaty laughter.
A perfume maybe. I probably imagined that.

Getting the rod down would be giving in.
The twisting, the yearning in the hands.
The dipping, the pulling tug.
Would it point to his field across the way?

Who would I be doing it for? The cattle?
The wind blows toward them
carrying the smell of water, and you can see them
grinding out a thick-tongued rumination,
debating the resistance of the barb wire.

At nights I roll in a torn sleep listening
to that stick chattering against the wall,
the wind hissing through the dry cotton,
and my cow's low moan.

MELTED CRAYONS

On the really cold mornings in the parish building basement
after the Sunday school lesson was over and before church started,
unbeknownst to the teacher,
me and the other boys would melt crayons into pools
on the flat top of the metal butane heater.

Then we would take a length of chalk from the board
and, in a practical application off the Coat of Many Colors I suppose,
we would roll that white stick through those pools,
slow to make the liquid stick,
but fast before the crayon cooked,
until we had what we thought was something clever
and wholly original in its dual purpose
that we knew we would never use because they were all works of art.

And then, driven by the bell, full of giggles and blushes,
we would go over to church, our minds filled with the thought of it,
all secret and waxy.
We would finger it and play with it in our pockets,
our brains too full of the swirling color and white dust
to absorb even a word of the sermon,

fidgety to finally be home, off in our secret place,
so that we could snap our creations asunder,
anxious to see what greasy pictures, what soaked glyphs,
what stains we would find inside the white bone.

HELD FOR THE BRIEF INSTANT FOREVER

There should be a relief of it,
something you can rub your hands over
so a blind man could know;
it should be tooled into a purse
or leather saddle—

but how to capture it?
how to make the kitchen clock stop
        when it never truly does,
how to capture the thrumming from the worm stick
that makes the nightcrawlers rise,

how to trace a new hoof print
and make it stay, lines fresh, untrammeled?
How can you do it,
what dies and stamps can you use,
what faith can you find in the leather?

How can you capture the steam from the stock tank,
a cottontail in mid-hop, the dog yawning,
the drumming thunder under a sheet metal roof,
the sun spilling over
and tilting the morning-glories?

What stitches can you use to bind the shapes?
What cut of the cowhide, what clasps, what bangles?
How can you make sure that
this moment does not escape you?
How can you hammer it in?

PAINTED ON A BARN

in large letters was the word PIG.
I could clearly read the word from the road.
There was nothing about "For sale" or "Farm."

What compulsion drove a man to label something so?
Did his wife have a special embroidered apron
with the word WOMAN emblazoned?

(Or, during those intimate hours,
did she have a girdle where her title would expand
horribly large in lycra?)

Or maybe this was just a casual, derogatory remark
aimed at no one in particular, maybe just at God,
to express a fleeting state of mind, a heretofore repressed enmity?

Or maybe it was a warning, a desperate feeble attempt
to make us stay away, to keep driving,
to make us think, make us tremble,

to keep us away from the gnawed pen, the erupted door, the smell
of musky, muddy, crushed furniture, the hoof-scratched tiles,
the final red glimpse of a terrible porcine slop.

SELECTIONS FROM
Translating the Prairie

SMALL POX EPIDEMIC

1895

It is dark here. Perhaps I have a story left to tell before I can move on although I always understood the innocent were led to God's right hand before all others. I am the daughter of Milt Collinsworth and I will only speak briefly and then step aside. We were trying to be hospitable to the peddler by putting him up for the night. An act of charity so rudely repaid. Did he know he was sick? He is not here to speak—but there are many behind me who are ready to. When he left I changed his bed liner. I quickly sickened. And died. But even then the goods the peddler had left were still working. (I am sorry, Mother and Father). At my funeral people crowded into my parents' small house—but the foul airs waited for them and went home with them, holding on with bony and claiming hands to their mourning clothes. The doctor was a fool—and I could only watch as others succumbed. There was a quarantine and roadblock. Then my family had to watch. And wait. And live alone. Even after the contagion was past. It is dark here. I have relatives behind me waiting to speak. We were innocent and isolated. We all have a story to tell.

THE EARTH

Early 1800's

Fragrance rises off the unturned fields
like a perfume that must surely permeate
the very fields of paradise. O stars, whose
view is pure and straight and is not bounded
by the earth's curve: tell me what do you see.
What censer of rain and sun and loam and river
swings to and fro, makes the wild daffodils burst,
fills the earth with mystic smoke and scented air
that wisps, that tendrils, that blows to me?

Yes, I smell it, as sure as drunk men smell gold.
The bouquet of crush berries, the birds wild with juice,
the quail exploding, the warm feathery air under their wings
as warm and seductive as the mist that lifts
from the springs that burble from the stones, from the blessed stones.

And I hear it.
I hear the foxes scurry, the buffalo drum the ground,
the birds soothing the pathway of their wings with song.
It is a song full of sirens, pulling the ship of my life.
There, westward, two weeks by wagon,
I will guide the schooner of my soul.
The earth there is calling.
I smell it.
I hear it.

THE GREGORY STALLION

Approximately 1920

The burnt flash on the gaskin.
The stippling on the quarters.
The crest wind-swept.
The sturdy chitinous hooves.
The broad-beam chest.
The prickled ears, the gaping maw of nostrils.
The barrel and the muzzle.
The tall and statured pose.
I will draw your eye away from all of that
to my right rear leg,
pointed downward and to the earth,
anxious to tear the turf,
to gallop,
to thunder.

SELECTIONS FROM
Smurglets Are Everywhere

THEY'RE EVERYWHERE!

Mr. Bibbles, rare inventor,
built a smurg madigulator
and it generated smurglets
on a fanduloso scale.

There were smurglets bright and twirmy.
Some were tall and some were swirmy.
Some were spotted, some were flappled,
and some even had a tail.

Mr. Bibbles, in elation,
took an overjoyed vacation
for his smurg madigulator was
a bambulous success.

But he left the darn thing running.
It kept running, running, running,
and it kept on making smurglets
which is why we're in this mess.

They saw they were unshackled.
They smooted and they brackled.
They frew and trew, and smackled
on their little dippled feets.

The smurglets kept on coming
'til the very walls were humming,
and they grabbled through the doorways,
and they poured into the streets.

Now there's smurglets doing taxes,
painting houses, getting waxes.
They are drippling from the gutters.
They are coming out the hose.

There are smurglets in the sockets,
deep in everybody's pockets,
and that's why there are smurglets
bathing in your fruity-o's.

THE EXHAUSTED WOODPECKER

He tried and tried and tried and tried.
He tried and tried and tried.
He tried and tried and tried and tried
and tried and tried and tried.

He tried and tried and tried and tried
and tried and tried and tried.
Perhaps we should have told him that
the tree was petrified.

WELDON WING THE ARMPIT KING

Weldon Wing the Armpit King
could really make his armpit sing.
His underarm had such a toot
you'd want to stand up and salute.

Birthdays, weddings, foreign guests—
He played for them—and did requests!
He's ambi-pits-trous so you'd see
him use both hands for harmony.

Something tender for your Mom?
He'll squeeze one out with such aplomb
that it will make your Mother sigh
and dab at something in her eye.

He went and had a CD made
to play for friends in second grade:
a treasury of greatest hits
which he entitled "It's the Pits."

Whatever the event demands
he's got the perfect pits and hands.
Bar mitzvahs, banquets—anything!
Call Weldon Wing, the Armpit King!

NEW POEMS
Non-Southwest

FOURTEEN MILES TO HEAVEN

The road sign is deceptive.
It is probably more like sixteen or seventeen miles to the heart of Heaven.
You have to drive through the suburbs of Heaven first.

That's the way mileage signs are.
We all accept that. It's tough enough to predict
the end of the world, especially down to a certain day,
but getting it down to a decade, heck, a millennium,
is in itself pretty impressive.
And even hinting we could have it down
to absolute feet—that's pretty boggling.

The problem with these vague mileage signs
is you don't really know when you're there
because you don't know when you started.
Or, in this case, when you finally hit the fourteenth mile.

Well, you could use an odometer.
We've all done that.
You could look around and say, yup, that gas station or that sidewalk
or that white cat strolling by staring at us is Heaven. Must be.
And now we are driving past the white cat
and the gas station and the sidewalk
so we must have passed through Heaven.

You start paying attention to what's on the other side.
It doesn't look like there are any zoning laws.
Goats roam the streets.
The lampposts are dark.

A TOAST TO THE ROGUE PIT BULL WHO TERRORIZES MY NEIGHBORHOOD AT NIGHT

How easily it all comes,
the insecurity like a thin blanket,
the agreement in the brain in the daylight
in the supermarket by the day old baked goods
to buy the cheaper wine
because after a while
all things are the same and there is no measure;
it's the rationalization that city glow
will mask any far-off defining speck that Tycho ever saw
with his naked eye.

This is how it comes then, the giving in to things,
the gentle erosion of courage,
the sloughing off of the markers of time.
how we learn to depend on the radio, the phone,
the ice cream truck.
At night I see the shadows of my neighbors
in their living rooms. They have given in.
Chaos is outside in the darkness.
Order is inside, and it's soothing.
And the sheets are clean and warm.

But tonight I am raising a glass to you,
dread pit bull, all speed and fiery bark.
You who run through these streets at night
like an uncharted comet.

The full moon is rising, tonight, just to the left,
at the end of the street, over the railroad tracks.
I am not so dull yet I have forgotten to look.

Tonight, like Tycho, I am willing to stand here,
in the dark, in my front yard, where the view is best.
This glass is raised to you, demon,
you ignorant slavering growl.
You are not immutable.
Tonight I am willing to lose my nose
for something as simple
as a clearer view.

A BIT PRESUMPTUOUS

It would probably be the height of entitlement
to ask Death if we might have a little notice.

It isn't as if I'm asking a lot.
I mean, I've already decided where my neighbors,
most of my relatives, and me,
are going after we die.

Destination, or lack thereof,
seems to be one of those theological points
no one really has much problem with,
even if some of us have decided there isn't a 'next-stop.'

But getting back to the notice thing:
It's like planning to leave on a trip to the beach.
We work backwards on the clock,
subtracting as we think of more things.
Hmmm, fifteen minutes to load the car,
half an hour to take a shower,
fifteen minutes to make coffee and grab a quick breakfast
(I have never heard of Charon also being a barista),
laying out the clothes, making lists to relatives,
maybe calling up a girlfriend
who jilted us in high school and saying hi!,
making sure the cat has plenty of water
until the house-sitter shows up.
So, that's two hours or so. Give or take.
I'm not locked into a specific amount of minutes.
Say, ninety then. That seems fair.
I understand that this appointment
isn't like a class we can skip.
I'm not negotiating for a permanent deferral.
I've read one too many stories about that.

No, it's like it's prom night and God is dad
and you've borrowed the car
and you have this mental checklist
of drink the punch, laugh too loud,
dance badly, kiss your date, squeeze her breast,
and still get home by curfew.

Why, even the stars can be tracked.
But are you saying that death isn't like the planets
but more like little meteorites
that are dusting the Earth everyday,
something we just can't ever keep track of there are so many,
falling all the time?
Why, that's just crazy.
I have my canopic jar of an ice chest loaded,
sitting by my chair.
My keys are in my pocket
and my wallet is full of cash.
It might be nice to have a sense
of how long the trip will be
but I'm as prepared as I'm gonna get.
It's time to just sit down in the comfortable chair,
take a deep breath,
watch the minutes burn away,
and wait to see what happens next.

ALMOST KNOWING WHAT WE KNOW

*…but the fact that the largest number of early symbolic
artifacts cluster around the fifty-thousand-year mark
doesn't mean that humans weren't symbol users
before then. As scholars like Terrence Deacon point out,
the absence of evidence is not evidence of absence.*
      The First Word—Christine Kenneally

When we were young and at Vacation Bible School
and we were pouring plaster of Paris into a mold
that was more than likely either a dog,
a cat, or the Lord's Prayer,
then two final acts were always required:
we needed to insert a sturdy wire hanger
into the upper back so that the item,
whatever it was, could be hung later.
And, secondly, the teacher made us
scratch our initials into the back of the almost dry plaster of Paris.

When real school finally started and we were handed
our primer the very first day
then the teacher would always tell us to open it
and look inside the cover
and to write our name and the year
on the little graph where the students in previous years
had written theirs. Everybody always hesitated,
reading the history of prior classes first, proud and scared
to join their ranks. Then, everybody would write their name
with too big a letters and wouldn't want to show anyone else.

In P.E. the coaches all said we had to have our initials
written inside our own gym clothes. In case there was ever
any arguments about socks or shirts or anything.

I stand here on the patio now, sipping my coffee,
wondering when I actually said my first word.
My mother has told me I was one when I said the word "hot."
I do not think it was the word "hot" at all
although I will admit her memory is probably clearer than mine.

I am just coming in from a long trip.
my suitcase is sitting by the front door,
the address tag tight around the handle.

I think we write our names in our Bibles
so we can harbor the illusion
that God knows who we are
and what we have studied,
when we finally show up.

We build in our own obsolescence without meaning to.
Plaster of Paris is just gypsum and it breaks down.
we outgrow our school clothes,
and there were only ten lines in the front covers of those books.

The decal on this coffee cup used to say
World's Greatest Dad.
It has worn away.

ECONOMICS

This morning the words were cooking slower
than the coffee maker, slower than a watched toaster,
so I let my eyes drift over to a poetry magazine I had bought.
You know the type. There is usually only one on any newsstand
at any one time, almost always a different one,
some digest sized thing with some
very literate phrase for a title,
and an artsy cover listing the names of authors
you have never heard of.

But inside this magazine I picked up
there was an article, very self-referential it seemed to me,
that said: The reading of poetry in the past ten years
has dropped over thirty percent.

I am not necessarily sure how that could even be measured.
Are there focus groups—or is it strictly based on sales numbers?
Were there interviews?
It might be just a matter of economics.
Even in the most golden of times
poetry books still fall way below the necessity of
movie tickets, new phones,
or any one of twelve kinds of decadent olives
a person dips for themselves at the grocery store.
It's true there was probably not a lot of poetry reading
during the Black Death. Who had time?
Everybody was out trying to run away from the foul vapors.
But now? Well, the last few years I suppose
have been a little thin for everybody.

Still, it was a relief to read the article.
Now, suddenly, I could rationalize
why my poems had been selling less and less.
It wasn't my fault at all, not an erosion of skills.
and I could hardly blame the editors either
who I had started labeling, all of them,
as moronic, uneducated twits.
They could not buy my poetry
because no one was buying any poetry. It was simple.
Well, that bitter pill went down a lot smoother now
(with a cup of brewed-by-myself-at-home coffee.)

But my dear, what this means
is that if things have become so austere
that even poetry, the humblest and lowest of needs,
(right below bad beer but, I hope, still right above
day-old French fries)——
as I say, if even the consumption of poetry has been pared back
then perhaps we must also consider cutting back
certain other things certain percentages.

The yard. I think mowing the yard.
I propose to mow it twenty-five percent less.
That can mean one of two things. I either mow it
twenty-five percent less often——
or I mow seventy-five percent of it very well, on schedule,
and let twenty-five percent of it go back to nature as it were.
I leave the choice up to you.

Nothing should be left off the table.
Birthdays, Mothers Day and Fathers Day.
Those are four potentials. I vote we only celebrate three of them
in any one year. We can put all the dates in a hat and draw blindly.
When that ignored day arrives,
we will sit in the backyard all day and talk about the weather.
When it gets dark we will immediately go to bed
so as to save electricity.

And speaking of bed, as I obliquely was,
It also means, my dear, that I will be kissing you
perhaps fifteen percent less.
(I am only human after all).
If I were you I would no longer count on
the peck on the cheek on your way to bed,
or the amorous smooch after three glass of wine.
I am not sure we can afford it.

There will also be a considerable cut back
in metaphoric speech, a trimming of allusions,
and a reduction in quotes, exact or paraphrased.

I feel confident all these numbers
will work their way back up again

as soon as things are,

literally and figuratively,
more flush.

SIMPLE REQUEST

"What do you want for Father's Day?"
I was asked. And the questioner knew
I have real issues with fake holidays
and people always expecting to buy or get something.

But there the question was, hanging now in the air between us,
like a piñata just waiting to get whacked,
so I whiffed at it and said, "Nothing really.
Seeing the kids. Maybe grilling some hot dogs."

Spin spin tighten the blindfold whack whack.
This was a verbal maneuver we knew pretty well,
so she said, "Is there anything you'd like to have
you wouldn't normally get for yourself?"

So I sat down and pretended I was thinking
and then said, "The other day at the grocery store
some woman asked me, because I was tall,
to reach a box of tea on a high shelf.

And she was pretty and she was showing a little cleavage,
and she had a voice that was a little musical,
not wonderfully melodious, but like something you hear on the radio
once every few years and you say,

"Oh yeah. That was a good song" and then you forget it.
Well, I'd like it if she had asked me my name,
and, right there, tea in hand, invited me out for coffee somewhere,
say, in an hour, in a place we both knew was quiet and safe.

And I would glance briefly at her cleavage and say,
"Please don't change before you get there."
And she would say, smiling back,
"Don't get shorter."

I took a deep breath, almost tasting the coffee.
"That is something I would like but not normally get for myself."
One two three one two three.
I had obviously connected with the piñata

but it wasn't the candy she expected.
"I'll just tell the kids to buy you a shirt."
I dislike holidays where we are expected to say what we want.
I prefer joys more serendipitous.

SNOW

When the little brother dropped his woolen hat
 into the flowing, snowy stream
(with his little sister saying, "He was leaning on the rail,
just like you told him NOT TO!")
then the bunch of kids, and me, and the girlfriend,
threw ourselves at the effort of rescuing the hat
with long sticks, off the steep, ten-foot-high bank.
It was no use. No stick was going to be long enough.
Right now the hat was hung on a branch
and that water was flowing at a good clip.
A few more minutes and it wouldn't be worth the chase.
The water wasn't deep, but it was a matter of getting to it
without falling in and everybody had an opinion
who we could afford to take a chance with.
It wasn't my hat so I choose not to vote.
I didn't know any of those kids, we could have lost one
and I couldn't have told the difference,
but the kids (who seemed to be multiplying like breads and fishes)
already had a plan and my girlfriend had
deep rain boots so there was this young girl, maybe twelve,
who was willing to negotiate down the slope into the water.
You'd have thought the hat was a kitten.
It was twenty degrees outside
but it was only a hat, for chrissakes.
The water had to be cold but the girl slowly worked her way over
and got it. I was one of the chain of hands that helped
pull the girl out. And then all the kids disappeared
like elves. As far as I know the river didn't
try to claim any more hats that day.

That night it snowed some more.
It covered up all the traffic marks
the kids had left. It hid the bushes, the steps,
and all the firewood it could reach.
My girlfriend and I broiled some steaks, opened some wine,
and then opened more wine. We turned off all the lights,
and raised the shades to see the glow of the snow.
We started kissing like it was a first date with no stop sign.
In the dark, with wine, there's no reading the other person's eyes,
A person forgets that night has an end.

It's what you have to do.

In the morning the people we were last night were gone.
She could see my eyes and I could see hers.
The sun was filling the room from the shades we had never closed.
She started making coffee; I stood by the door.
Why, sure, I said, there is the bridge and the rail,
and if you listen closely you can hear the stream.
She tilted her head, listening, and smiled a little.
There was a tiny spot of dried wine on her lip.
We leaned toward each other,
unbalanced over the kitchen counter,
tried to remember from years ago
our parents' warning.

BASEBALL

She told me to write a love poem about baseball
that did not mention bats or green grass
or home runs.
So, I said, baseball is like dogs defying gravity
when they leap for butterflies.
It's like the quiet of small, dark, wooden rooms
when the light comes in slices,
when the pen sits in your hand,
and you hold your breath waiting
for the perfect phrase to just come OH!

Baseball is like kissing the right girl. It starts out
as a quiet thing that turns into a loud thing,
a very loud thing, a roaring in the ears,
that sends out waves that resonate out
to some lonely pile of stones in Italy, or maybe Tibet,
and maybe it vibrates just enough to dislodge a stone
to reveal a lost scroll that has one word, one word is all it takes,
a word that makes all the difference.

It's a word that could never ever have happened until now,
starting out in silence. turning into a roar.
Like a perfect kiss. That lets us defy gravity.
That keeps us holding our breath OH!

CONTINUOUS AS THE STARS THAT SHINE

This morning I am sitting here with my hot coffee
and I am looking through the window out across my yard,
the yard that has no fence,
the yard that disappears into tangles of trees and high grass.
I have a manuscript beside me,
and an idle pen,
and an eye that is searching for a focal point.
I know that summer's heat has already built up
into the concrete patio outside my window
that the owner thrice-removed had poured
because he wanted to be a lawn-chair length closer
to his focal point of trees and high grass.
I know that the heat is already deep enough into that concrete
that it will not fully dissipate until perhaps November,
and that between now and then the patio
will be practically unlivable to everything except patio furniture.
But now I am sitting here in the cool,
at my breakfast room table,
and I am thinking of fulfilling a friend's request
to write a cover blurb for his manuscript.
It isn't as if a blurb is like a review,
something for academics to read,
some obscure words to be buried on the last page of the op-ed section.
This is somewhat bigger than an ad saying New And Improved,
and it is certainly is not as tender or money-filled as
a greeting card for a graduate.
And it is nowhere close to Moses coming down
carrying a stone volume spread apart saying, "Read This Book!"
No. It is a cover blurb, a funny-sounding noun
that sounds like a cartoon character drowning.
It is a word balloon without borders,
an epigram full of promises and hope and extra dessert.
But like the heat that has slowly built up on my patio
I have read this manuscript slowly. Here I liked this bit about stars,
who doesn't like stars, but I could not understand his comparisons

of stars to vegetables and some fruit Eliot mentioned.
And something else I do not understand is that
in the first third of the book
daffodils have been mentioned at least twelve times.
There may be people who like daffodils
as much as they like stars but I am afraid that group is limited
to people who like Wordsworth. Or astronomers who yearn for eclogues.
Still, I can only think that the home-owner thrice-removed
and my author friend and those people who might be
wondering lonely as a cloud deserve a little something.
I see the heat waves rising from the stone, and tap my fingers
on the next poem (which I can already see contains more daffodils)
and I say a tiny prayer that perhaps
I have missed a news story about a little Ice Age
that any hour now will glacially invade my acreage.
It will create a Nordic horizon in the tangle of trees,
and make tundra of my yard,
until it finally reaches my patio, the patio that never gets cool.
And then it will cover that.
And then it will slowly break the windows into my breakfast room,
and I will offer it this manuscript,
and I will watch in a kind of joyous despair
as it pulls it page by page into its icy maw.
And after it has finally consumed the 'about the author' page
then I will step away with my now cold cup of coffee
and I will call the publisher to claim the manuscript was lost.
Then I and my breakfast room will disappear into history
for that is what Time and Tastes and Focal Points do.
And that is why decades, maybe centuries, from now,
when the ice has started to retreat,
then future poets, with their parkas and their steaming cups of coffee,
will say, with a delight I could never raise,
"Here. Let us lay down on this cool concrete slab.
And look at this ice over here!
It is full, full of daffodils!"

DEATH GOES COURTING

Damn how he kept getting reimagined.
Things were much easier in the Charon days:
there was always money in the bank,
People came to him, all he had to do was row, row, row.
And then there was the heyday of the Black Death.
Well, sure, he'd been mis-portrayed on the tarot cards,
there was that, (and Lord knows every cliché of a gypsy
and bad horror writer had come to depend on that interpretation),
and it still made him feel queasy remembering the day
when the x-ray was invented. It was like looking at himself
In the mirror Every. Single. Day. But Death was Death. And
He was Death. And everything wore out and got ground down
or burned up or torn up or made into something else.
There was no moral compass to it, regardless of how
he was illustrated. He had checked once and nope, there was
no umbilicus that attached a soul to a skeleton. He had looked all over,
checked each patella and phalange.
God and Soul and Death—all separate things.
Man never did get it, never could reconcile it,
always wanted to put some extra meaning on it,
flesh it all up with emotion, make it softer, ease everyone into it.
So, here he was, trying to look as dignified as possible,
(were his ribs straight?), flowers in one hand,
teeth showing as friendly as possible, about to let this woman know,
in his socially inconvenient way,
how seriously he planned on dating her,
how he was intent on making her his own.

THE AUCTION COMPANY

They made it very clear
they would not consider selling
any painting done on velvet.

The first thing
that comes to mind
is all the Elvis poses
that would be orphaned.
And then after that
all the Unicorns.

This type of discriminatory behavior
has the sublimely understated
subtext of a
demarcation of taste.

"No, we will never bring out
a grilled cheese sandwich. Or fries.
And certainly not a chocolate shake,"
said the chef at the
snooty French restaurant.

"Nor will we serve any wine
with the word Ripple in the title.
Or any other wine that is named after
a belligerent canine."

There must have been
a velvet rope of sorts
to be an artist
in the caves of Lascaux.
You had to have at least seen
an auk.

No second-hand stories.
No tales heard from a friend of a friend.
"Here, draw one in the dirt.
No, an auk does not have wings."

It's almost as if
Grandpa had purposely kept
a Picasso in the attic

because he liked the way the face
seemed to be looking
all directions at once.

And contrary to what
some folks will tell you
on the Entrance to Heaven form
there is no blank marked:
Religion.

At some point
it's no longer a question of value.
We don't need to be Thomas
Or Lot. Or Pharaoh.

It's the river rising
and carrying all the coffins downstream.
It's digging down so deep
there's no trace of us beyond that point.

There's only the reaching out
with our breath held
and our eyes closed
and being able to touch
the always-fuzzy beard
of God.

IMPASSE

Compromise
has no meaning to the snake
who is curled
under the stalks.

The black opalescence
of his eye
compels us to be
obsequious.

His attitude says,
"We have met here
and now I own your steps.
I will latch onto your ankle.
Do not move."

How easy it is
for the crow
to hop from ear to ear,
nibbling, ignoring all boundaries,
only scared with a shoo.

Here, in this shaded corner,
different rules apply.
There are parameters.
Our breath is slave to this ophidian glare.

If only walking away
would solve this rattling conundrum,
would shatter us from
our icy temerity.

We're past prayers.
It will take bigger words than we know
to free us now,
a bigger hoe than we carry.

Until those syllables are voiced
we stand here and sweat,
the commands of the snake
hissing in our captive ears.

INEXHAUSTIBLE

I shall stop complimenting you as of this hour.
I have already used up all my praising words for today.
I spent them talking to the courageous rabbit who nibbles in my yard.
I told the grackles in the alley down the street their sheen was opalescent.

Yes, there is a ration of words. Are we so romantic
as to believe we can generate uplifting words forever,
even when our lips are thin and sere,
and muscles no longer cling to any parts of us,

when we go to bed
and our hands already assume a prayer pose,
our face tilted up to the ceiling
ready to humbly kiss the cheeks of angels?

Tomorrow morning I will write words about you, save them,
and store them in a safe place for later use.
In a closet, in a sealed container, I plan you will find whole phrases
that will describe alone the softness of your neck.

But tonight, when I am thinking too much of endings
you will utter a syllable only lovers understand.
Your breath will quicken me.
I will borrow against the future.

GUIDE

Here. Let me restack the wood on your porch.
It does not need restacking but it is unsymmetrical.
A new order will make for a purer picture of where you live
for anyone who is walking by.

Allow me to rake the snow before you. It is a foolish thing.
Stay my hand on the wooden handle.
I am small and presumptuous for thinking and wanting
to smooth your path.

I will help you hang candles this afternoon.
This may be what God intended.
The stars are there all the time.
They are better beacons when we are darkest.

ONLY ONE POEM PER PAGE

It isn't like haiku
where you can stack stanzas
like seventeen-syllable cordwood.

No, according to this journal,
if in your submission
you put more than one poem on a page
then there is evidently
the wondering where one thing ends
and the other begins—
like having to take both your girlfriend
and her prettier step-sister to the prom.

Please understand that I
am not taking sides here.
I am not advocating poetry
where all the lines arrive simultaneously
like second-graders.

But I rather like road-trips
where sometimes one town leads to another.
They might even be close by,
so close where neighbors are in different postal codes.
Not always. But sometimes.

But evidently, and, I am afraid
unbeknownst to most poets,
what can happen
is that the editor will rip open the envelope
and his eyes,
normally expecting the white chasm of a page break,
will simply find a leap-able gap.

Rather than be intrigued,
he will be distracted by the second poem.
Lines from the first poem may still be
on the tip of his tongue
But like two radios playing at once
he will lose the ability to distinguish.

That editor will spend the rest of his day
blind to the personal space of things.
He will bounce off people in the elevators.
He will not walk in straight lines.

The poor editor will go home to his wife.
At dinner, where he has not tucked in his napkin,
he will find himself
hopelessly not knowing where the peas stop
and the pork chop starts.

One part of him
will see his wife
in her pleated and well-bound glory.

And another part of his brain
will be full of,
and only full of,
the name of his first girlfriend.
He will desperately try to forget
the color of her eyes.

BE THANKFUL FOR

Before hot chocolate
folks might have sat around saying
"Let's have a cup of water and dirt."

That person who invented hot chocolate,
probably some Mayan,
deserves his own time of recognition.
like a literary festival,
where everyone would sit around
making smores
and reciting poems about marshmallows
and grandmas
and feeling cozy in winter.

In this parsimonious age
maybe it would be enough to give him
at least one waking hour.
Say, 3 p.m. every second Saturday of January.
Don't plan birthday parties then.
We will all be drinking cocoa.

It may be too much to ask
but I would also like to have a festival
for the grackle that occupies the elm
outside my bedroom window every morning.
He lies to me and tells me
that the sun has been up for hours.
Lying, telling the truth—it is all the same to him.

And, since I am talking about
filling up the stations of the day
I will also personally set aside
a few minutes of time
for a memory of minnows.
Once, when I was fishing
I saw a school of them
in a shallow, sunny spot
next to a partially submerged log.

They seemed to hang suspended
in the clear water,
like tiny piscine angels,
waiting in the glowing
to grow just a little more,
their putti bodies quivering silver,
their tiny mouths circular
in wondrous hunger.

JUST IN PASSING

Maybe one last thing maybe could be said:
Words. Words are what I did.
Prior wives, girlfriends,
mentors, people reading my books—
I would give you a message if I could
when I am performing my final hovering,
but by then I will have already learned a new tongue,
even more exquisite
than the language of Taa
with its thirty-one vowels.
Even so,
I promise I will still try
to speak your name
when praise is all I know.

PHLOX

Short prayer penetrates heaven
—The Cloud of Unknowing

In just a few words then
I will describe the small,
purple flowers blooming
in my yard, reaching for
the sun, defying me
to mow them down. "Look up,"
they say. "Look up. The sun
is warm. And your roots are
not half as deep as ours."

AT THE LIQUOR STORE THE OTHER DAY

I stood in front of the Irish Whiskey display
looking for an elusive brand
that I have read about
in articles that use superlative terms.
It does not seem to exist.

Based on what I have read on the internet
there are lots of mature women
who want to date men exactly my age.
Some of them want long-term relationships;
some of them want to be discreet;
some evidently live in my neighborhood.
I have not seen anyone who matches the pictures.

The type of Irish Whiskey I am looking for
does not live in my neighborhood,
although I know it does exist.
I have read about it
in articles that use superlative terms.
I am not sure this type exists
in this state, country, or continent.

I am thinking that one of the women
who wants to date me is right now at the grocery store,
pushing her cart alone,
or perhaps she is getting her oil changed
because she is, after all, a mature woman.
She might as well be in another country.

A salesman at the liquor store comes up
and tells me that the Queen of England
drinks a particular brand that is on sale.
It is a brand I have never heard of before.
I doubt that the Queen of England and I
will ever meet publicly over a glass. I would imagine
she would prefer a discreet relationship.

At the end of the day
one of the women who wants to date me
has undone one too many buttons on her pajama top,
has curled up on her sofa,
and is preparing to watch a movie
that was talked about in superlative terms.
She may hear a noise outside,
maybe even a hopeful knock on the door,
but she will decide it is nothing really,
and then go on watching the moving pictures
in her totally royal way.

GOODNIGHT SWEET PRINCE

My mother and father
would always tell me
to say my prayers right
before I went to sleep at night.
At some point they also told me
to count sheep.
I was never sure
how the two processes were related.

As I grew older,
and thought I had exhausted
the efficacy of prayer,
I would wind down my day
by reading.
Then, when my eyes were too tired,
I would look at the page of where I was,
and the last page of the book,
close my eyes, and, in my head,
do the percentage math problem of what I had read,
all the way out to four digits if I had to.

I could have said I recited
the first two hundred digits of pi.
But that's an old problem
and the numbers never change.
Page counts marked progress,
let me know, reassuringly,
how far I had come.

I am envious of angels
who are good at math.
I suspect many of them
can do percentages
up to ten decimal places, maybe fifteen.

Maybe they could even count
all the sheep there are,
all the prayers,
all the pages in all the sleepy books.

LE MUSÉE DU DUST BOWL

After Auden——and inspired by "Fleeing a dust storm",
Arthur Rothstein, photographer, April, 1936

About dust they knew everything,
the sharecroppers: how well they understood
its presence, how it could scour a man to nothing
while someone else was driving dully along a highway.
How, when aged ears were listening
to tales of jobs and food there were always
children who had not grown up knowing what dreams were.
But they knew the martyrdom had to run its course
anyhow in some gritty tent, or a shack,
where the dogs went on with their thin lives or
a disconsolate man fell against a post.

In Rothstein's photo for instance, how the father
and his sons struggled against the wind, how we could imagine
a woman back east, eating apricot jam on toast,
who might have seen the photo but for her it was not
an important disaster. The sun shone,
as it had to, on her white legs disappearing into her sun dress
and the servant poured coffee from the expensive
silver pot. The photo showed only one small boy
being left behind after all. Besides, she had a meeting to get to
and her car was waiting impatiently downstairs.

THERE IS NO PIE ON MARS

There are no straight rivers nor perfectly straight coast lines in Nature's plan. So if it could be shown that there are long straight canals on Mars, that would be accepted as evidence of the presence of intelligent beings there.

Well, it is probably too late to tear down
Lowell's mausoleum then,

even if it has been proven,
as far as proof can go for a place we can't even drive to,

that the canals on Mars that Lowell talked about
were more wishful extrapolation than anything else.

Tearing down things named after people
who were later proven wrong, or at least not worthy,

has a long historical record.
There are a bunch of pharaohs

whose dynasties and names I can't remember, ever,
who sent teams around scratching

the prior pharaoh's name off stones,
so no one would be inclined to say,

"Oh yeah. I remember him.
I liked him better than what we have NOW."

We should have realized long ago
that really the whole burning topic

was about straight lines and perfect forms and how
the human mind tends to put them where they really aren't.

Yes, we impose order on brownies,
and lemon bars, and ice cream sandwiches

casseroles in square dishes,
processed cheese, sheet cakes.

Real estate inheritances.
Beds. Books.

Those are our marks of civilization;
the presence of intelligent beings

A pie-server for instance.
is designed, in shape, to serve the perfect wedge.

Grandmothers wield it with nurturing efficiency.
It would work in space,

a pie server big enough
could subdivide the stars,

a wedge of galaxy for each of us,
Yummy, still hot at the center.

But it's artificial. On Mars there is
no little diner you can stumble across

off the beaten path, just past the undeveloped crater,
where a many-tentacled waitress named Molene

would never serve the best bacon (in ill-formed ribbons),
or fried eggs (never poached), with sopping drop biscuits.

And for dinner you could never have martian-beast steak,
or martian mashed potatoes with martian banana pudding.

Or guacamole—as much as you would like but not get,
(because, as ubiquitous as it is, it would not exist on Mars.)

And there would never be pie.
Never any pie. They would always be out of pie.

No matter how much you would stare at the menu.
No matter how much you would whine from your
                                          perfectly square plastic booth.

URBAN EARTHQUAKES

Around here urban earthquakes
are like short city women
with tiny breasts.

They are cute, other women say,
but once they are passed
then they are gone, little fissures
barely remembered.

But fissures are fissures
and for most men
fissures are like a call to Mecca.

Metaphorically and mentally,
with even the slightest jiggle,
those men will fall to their knees
and hide under their desks.

But a man's man will ride it out,
stare it in the face,
maybe comb his hair while it's happening.

He'll be waiting for the large tremor,
an indigenous woman's breasts,
pendulous, hypnotic, and ready to cause
all manners of historical damage.

WEALTH

Do Not Regard Anything As Valuable That Can Be Taken Away
   —Seneca

Iron. Wood. Tin plates. A comfortable chair.
Good tea made from fresh water
that came from your well.
A handshake. The look in the face of someone
who is shaking your hand and means it.
A doughnut—a really good doughnut.
A fence tall enough to keep neighbors out.
Rules. Free pens. Your grandmother's love letters.
The first book you ever read.
A picture of you on a bicycle.
That moment you realized your best friend
had eyes a different color than yours.
Hand tools, like a hoe, or rake, or shovel.
The memory of cactus. Being slapped.
Falling off something. Getting the breath knocked out of you.
Remembering what being ashamed felt like.
Waving to someone across the street.
Asking for help. Being tired from staying up
too late playing dominoes.
Bathing in the Ganges. Wading in a stream
you have to check a map later to know the name of.
Ruining your shoes on purpose
 in the rainwater in the street.
Kissing badly but getting better at it.
Wondering how many treasures
are stored behind other people's doors and windows.
Being ready. Being ready to let go.
The Leopard's Spots. Wonder.

WHY I REMEMBER LITTLE BLACK SAMBO

*Sambo is a South Indian boy who lives with his father and mother, named Black
Jumbo and Black Mumbo, respectively. Sambo encounters four hungry tigers, and
surrenders his colourful new clothes, shoes, and umbrella so they will not eat him.
The tigers are vain and each thinks he is better dressed than the others. They chase
each other around a tree until they are reduced to a pool of melted butter. Sambo
then recovers his clothes and his mother, Black Mumbo, makes pancakes out of the
butter.*
—*Wikipedia*

If four women wanted to steal my clothes, and put them on,
and then start a circular cat fight about how they looked
I would probably have paid money for that. If it wasn't in my wallet.
In my pants. That one of the women was wearing.

Nothing here is about what MY name really is.
It's about menu and science. There isn't really a moral here either.
It's just a fairy tale with no happily-ever-after.
But maybe a lot of syrup.

Well, maybe there is a moral, but if stealing clothes and then
being vain and then being turned into butter is a moral
I'm thinking there is some transubstantiation connection
that has been misunderstood.

As for my role here, my first naked tendency
would be to say there has to be alchemy involved.
There had to be a philosopher's stone somewhere.
After the spectacle of course.

I would have liked to have a say as to what these women
would change into—although no version of the original story
seems to indicate Sambo had a choice.
But the rules dictate the adversaries have to change into something

so I'm thinking maybe a tall glass of a really good dunkel.
Maybe a pound of bacon. A gift basket full of lotions and soaps
(Black Mumbo would like that.) A bag of kettle popcorn.
A string of bratwursts tied end to end.

But no, history says that ultimately you will need
to be angry about me. There's not much mention made of the tigers
and how they were punished for their sin of pride.
All I did was show up well-dressed.

Give me the name you want—
but whatever those women turn into I'll still get my clothes back.
The real moral of the story is how
when women meet men everybody changes.

We pause, we dance, butter is usually involved,
there's reduction—we become something else.
Call me Sambo, call me an idiot to see women dancing.
But I will still take the path that is full of tigers.

NEW POEMS
Southwest

SOCIAL STUDIES, TEXAS SCHOOLS, LATE 1960'S

Mexico got no books, light bulbs, or electricity.
They got no hamburgers. They don't have milk, orange juice,
or Coca-Cola. They only have one kind of hat.

They have no history except Santa Anna.
Between Texas and South America is nothing.
They don't have mountains or deserts or river or lakes.

They have goats for pets.
Dogs stand on this side of the river and bark across.
They have cats there but they are all scrawny.

The women all wear fiesta-type dresses.
The women all have castanets.
The children have no shoes.

The men all have moustaches.
Everybody there drinks cheap beer. Even the babies.
They eat only tamales for breakfast, lunch, and dinner.

Every building has a mural painted on it
and the paint is chipping off. There are fountains in every yard
but none of them have water.

Every yard is full of cactus. There is no grass there anywhere.
They have schools but nobody goes.
All of the highways are only gravel.

They have cars there but they are all old.
Only the rich people have burros.
There are lots of snakes.

A lot of people live in villages.
Mexico City is the capital of Mexico.
Don't go there. It is next to a volcano.

I don't care what the maps say: there are no
beaches in Mexico. Nobody there has a good time.
They are all unhappy.

Stay on this side of the Rio Grande and just wave.
If you ever drive over into Mexico
you might never come back.

BABY CACTUS

City people love them
like they were puppies.
We could sell a thousand
if we had the pots.

They ask if we have a box to hold them.
They have no sense
of how to handle them
when they grow too big.

No way to tell them
some things can't be tamed,
that they just bought things
that live to pierce.

They'll discover soon enough
they can't let them stay inside,
not with all the babies,
not with bare feet in the darkness.

They are too wild to live in the house.
They'll consign them to the backyard,
discover what we already knew
with our hoes and shovels.

They'll try to hold them off best they can,
make them understand they can come
no closer than the fence line,
walking the edge, showing their yellow teeth.

LIVING SOUTH OF SONORA

It's a given the forms
your mind can attach a sound to.
We're taught each thing
has its own syllabus of noise.

Possums, raccoons, skunks—
they're huggers and pushers,
using their body and shoulders;
sniffing, washing—innocent diggers.

Most birds are just visiting
in a pecking kind of way.
Horned lizards bare-palm stones.
Prairie dogs dig with alert abandon.

All manners of creature:
even some man in the dark
that's lost and just shambling through—
your ear can prick and dismiss it.

But there are other noises you can't place:
maybe a screech or a loud scratch,
a branch that screams in bending—but doesn't break,
something that splashes where there isn't water.

Some noises you don't explore after.
You leave the night door shut.
The flashlight might reveal an odd glistening,
some shambling bulk that isn't afraid.

You decide you aren't ready to find
those things bold enough to give themselves away,
faces assimilated into the stones,
roots that don't mind being submerged.

There may be pools out there your feet aren't aware of,
currents full of strange phonics,
tassled with creatures floating at the right hand of mermaids,
waiting patiently for you to get lured in.

TALOS: THE WINDMILL

He points to the wind,
rooted in his duty,
in love with the earth and the sun.
He seems to ignore intruders.

Bound by green years and whim
he stands—a forged creation,
feet oozing ichor,
covered in verdigris.

He waits for Man and Fate.
He controls the water.
His tall eye sees everything.
His guardian blades slice the wind.

He only seems benign.
Let someone but disturb the air
and he will turn. The fools will hear
his tearing metal screech.

SELECTIONS FROM

Here We Measure Between Wings

SELECTION 1

We could never believe it's a flat earth here.
We've been up high enough on these out-croppings
to know the curves of Satan's body,

the muscular loins, the rolling chest,
the cable bones of his neck,
the way his head rounds up to the crown.

The higher we go the more there is.
There's a measureable distance
between the tips of Satan's wings.

Only God knows the number.
He has counted each step.

SELECTION 2

West of El Paso,
past the remnant oasis,
is where they say Satan fell.

If you climb to the top
of the tallest tree in town
you can just see the edges of the charred spot.

It's too hard to drive there.
You'll turn back when you lose hope.
Only angels dare fly over it.

Don't peer too long.
You'll imagine you see smoke rising
like breathing from a sentient abyss.

SELECTION 3

There's no point in
putting demons into the swine here.

These hogs are angry enough.
They root and charge like rabid dogs.

They were here right after the hawks
and they harbor a grudge about
sharing their bristly space.

There's no telling if they can die.
I suspect if I managed
to drive them off a cliff
they would simply land, roll,

then snort at me
over their foam-flecked shoulders,
torn tusks eviscerating the air,

squealing voices describing
all types of imagined slaughter.

SELECTION 4

Only once did I build
a fire outside at night.

That fire attracted mice,
drawn into the warm.

That brought in owls
from all parts of the darkness:
great sudden clouds
of brown and white and claw.

All I could hear were
small necks breaking.

All I could see were
the pentecostal embers
of tiny souls.

SELECTION 5

The spirit that's bedded out there
recognizes no magnetism,
sneers at tectonics,
ignores the perfect order.

Go ahead and wear icons;
It doesn't care.
Its eyes won't even roll.

It is far past any tidal pull
or metaphoric twig.

It can't be driven off.
It yawns at supplications.

It hardly notices
how things are crucified here
every day.

SELECTION 6

Between many of the low bushes
there are trails other animals
have formed. Why is it I think
their paths have not been erased
when my tracks are so easily scratched away?

Maybe if I could fly up high enough
I might see something more
in these mere creature's lines,

some hieroglyph, some symbolic language
that will never be translated
by a clouded human mind.

Perhaps the trail is only an accepted route,
some guided shallow furrows,
that high-up spell out
some unreadable name.